# MAKING
# MOVING
# TOYS

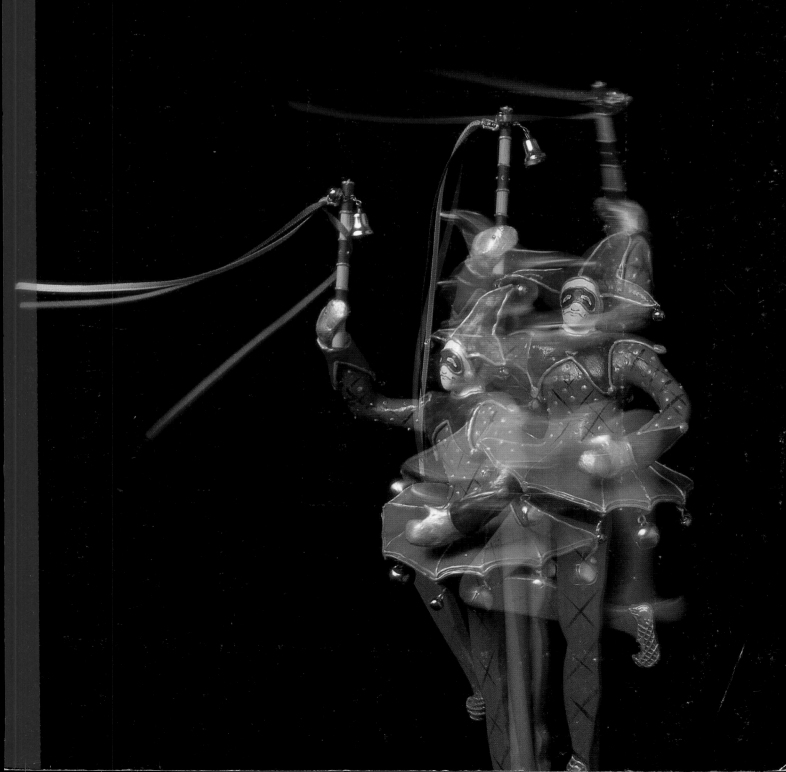

# MAKING
# MOVING
# TOYS

### 30 quick and easy projects to make

*Pippa and Ian Howes*

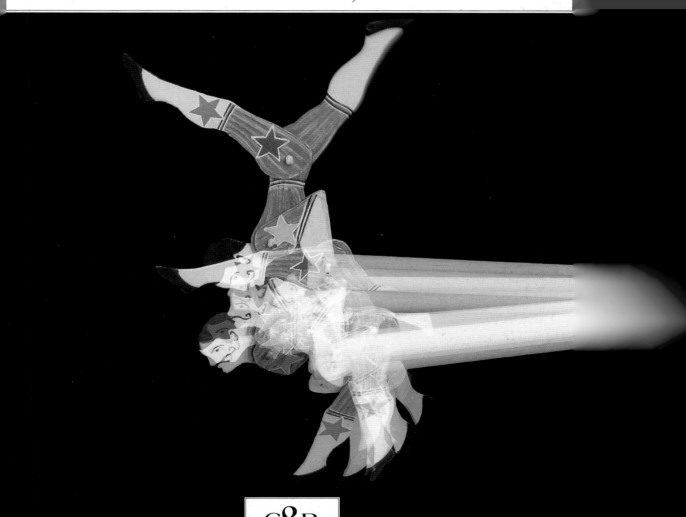

COLLINS & BROWN

T2T.
H839m
1999

First published in Great Britain in 1999 by
Collins & Brown Limited
London House
Great Eastern Wharf
Parkgate Road
London SW11 4NQ

9 8 7 6 5 4 3 2 1

British Library Cataloguing-in-Publication
Data:
A catalogue record for this book is available
from the British Library.

ISBN 1 85585 453 8

Editor          Kate Yeates
Designer        James Culver
Photography     Pippa and Ian Howes
Toymakers       Pippa and Ian Howes

Reproduction by H.K. Graphic and Printing
Printed in Hong Kong by Midas

Distributed in the United States and Canada
by Sterling Publishers Co, 387 Park Avenue
South, New York, NY 10016, USA.

# CONTENTS

# THE PROJECTS

# INTRODUCTION

In an age of mass produced plastic and electronic playthings, a handmade toy is a rare treat. Toys are fun to make and even more fun to give or receive as presents: there can be few things more rewarding than watching someone enjoying a toy you have made especially for them.

The desire to entertain as much as to please was the inspiration behind this book. As father and daughter our wish to come up with special treats (or bribes!) for the grandchildren/children led us to experiment with odd bits and pieces found around the house and the workshop. When you start looking, it's surprising what can be turned into a moving toy with a little ingenuity and a few household tools.

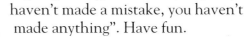

The projects are based on traditional toys with simple movements and have been successfully tried and tested on children young and old. The toys range from classroom favourites such as Paper Airplanes and Pop-up Baby, to more sophisticated models like The Woodchopper and Spinning Harlequin. Some toys, such as the Galloping Carousel and the paper Windmills are easy to make and children will love to help create them. Others like the Traditional Carousel and Drinking Cats demand more time, patience and craftsmanship but will doubtless be treasured for years.

All the projects are graded from easy to moderately easy to difficult so that you know before starting whether to attempt a particular toy straight away or try a slightly easier one first. Each project has clear step-by-step instructions to show you exactly what to do, and all the projects that need them have trace-off shapes for templates at the back of the book.

Whether you are a complete beginner or a skilled toymaker, we hope you will find projects that will inspire you and help develop your skills. Just have a go and don't worry about it going wrong, remember, "if you haven't made a mistake, you haven't made anything". Have fun.

# MATERIALS, TOOLS & TECHNIQUES

All the toys in this book can be made by anyone with patience and a few basic tools. Some of the projects are extremely simple and need little more than a pair of scissors, a piece of card and some crayons. Others are made from plywood and MDF, or sculpting materials, all of which are widely available in DIY stores or model makers' suppliers. Most of the tools used are those found in the average tool box such as a hammer, drill, saw and craft knife. As most people will be familiar with some but not all of the techniques used in the book, here we look at the general craft and woodworking techniques used to make the toys.

## WOOD, PLYWOOD AND MDF

These materials are perfect for toy making as they are hard wearing, easy to cut and shape, lightweight and provide a good surface for decorating. They can be bought from DIY stores, but it is worth trying a local wood yard first for offcuts which are often free. Although specific thicknesses are given for each project, there is a little leeway either side if you have a slightly thicker or thinner piece of wood, plywood or MDF.

Dowel rods and wooden balls are also widely available in DIY and hardware stores. As the thickness of dowel sold varies from store to store, again, do not worry if you use one a fraction bigger or smaller than that given in the project list. The point to remember is to always match the dowel size to the drill bit making the hole the dowel is to fit into. If in doubt, use a slightly bigger dowel and sand it down to fit in the hole.

## SAFETY

Safety is of paramount importance when working with wood and MDF. Always wear a dust mask and eye protection when cutting, drilling, or sanding as the dust created is hazardous. Work in a well ventilated room and always clear up with a vacuum cleaner when you finish. Take great care when using cutting tools and always use sharp blades in craft knives and saws as a blunt edge necessitates more force, and an accident is likely to happen. Read and follow the safety instructions in power tool manuals and make sure that power cables are kept well clear of saw blades and other sharp edges.

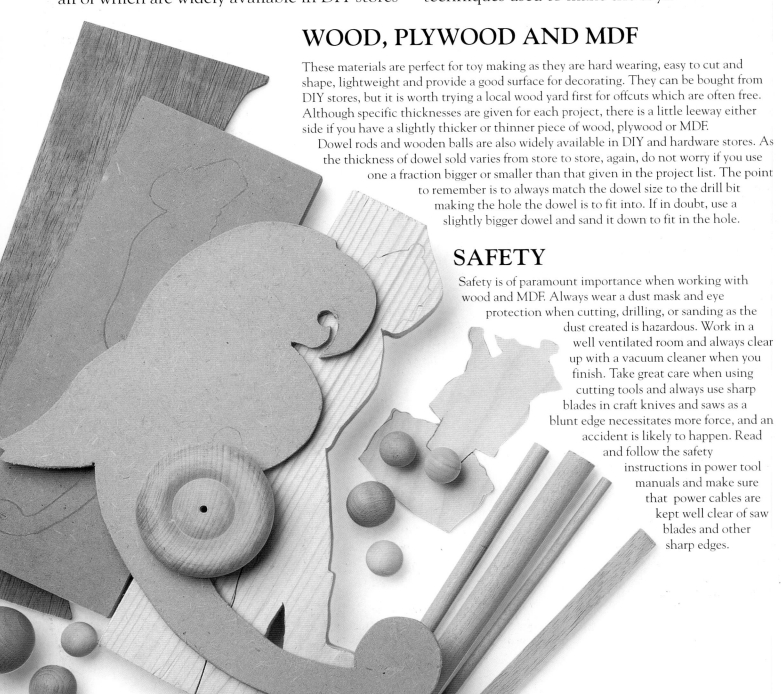

# CUTTING

The techniques covered here are the main ones used in the projects. When cutting a large piece of wood or MDF, make sure it is firmly clamped to keep it steady. Keep fingers well out of the way of the blade and never leave cutting tools lying around.

### CUTTING AN INTERNAL SHAPE WITH A JIGSAW

An electric jigsaw is excellent for cutting curves and circles. To cut out the centre of a shape, first drill a hole near the start of the cut for the blade to fit into. Jigsaws cut on the up stroke so make sure that the base of the saw is resting firmly on the material before starting. Let the motor reach full speed before starting to cut and try not to force the blade as it will clog up with sawdust and overheat. With some shapes it may be easier to hold the saw still and move the workpiece on to it. Jigsaws can also be used to cut a straight line – you will need to use a straight edge to guide the blade when doing this.

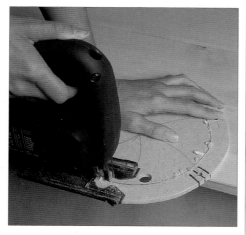

*Always keep hands well out of the way of the blade when cutting.*

### CUTTING WITH A FRETSAW

Fretsaws can be fitted with a variety of blades according to the thickness of the material you are cutting. A medium blade 8 teeth per centimetre (18 teeth per inch) has been used for all the projects in this book. Make sure you put the blade in the right way up – fretsaws cut on the down stroke. Clamp the work to the bench to hold it steady when cutting.

*Saw along the marked line, turning and reclamping the work regularly so you always cut in the same direction. Cutting out to the edge occasionally can make the piece of work easier to handle.*

*Fretsaw blades will always take the line of least resistance, so special care is needed when cutting softwood as the blade has a tendency to try to follow the grain. Always turn the work and not the blade.*

*To cut a hole or an internal shape, remove the blade from the fretsaw and thread it through a pre-drilled hole, reconnect it and saw along the marked line.*

## CUTTING TOOLS

There are numerous types of saws for cutting wood, and the range can be quite confusing. For the toys in this book you will need to cut straight and curved lines in a variety of materials. We use four types of saw; a cross-cut saw, a fretsaw, a junior hacksaw and an electric jigsaw. You could, however, get by without the jigsaw.

**Fretsaw** *Designed for making curved cuts in wood, plastic and other soft materials, it is one of the most important toymaking tools.*

**Junior hacksaw** *An inexpensive saw no toolbox should be without, it is very useful for cutting small items such as dowels, bolts and welding rods.*

**Cross-cut saw** *Used to cut straight lines in wood. Cutting plywood and MDF will quickly ruin the blade of a good saw, so it is advisable to use a cheap hardpoint saw and replace it with another when blunt.*

**Electric jigsaw** *This has interchangeable blades that can cut tight curves and circles, or straight lines in a variety of materials. Follow the manufacturer's guide to select the appropriate blade for the job.*

# CUTTING

## CUTTING THIN PLYWOOD

This material is easy to cut with a sharp, strong craft knife, however, be prepared to use a few blades as the points snap off with boring regularity. Always guide the blade against a straight metal edge and rest the workpiece on a cutting mat. When cutting slots it is easier to cut the long sides first, then push the blade into the corners to remove the narrow ends. Use sharp scissors to cut curves, they tend to leave a slightly rough bevelled edge, but this can be cleaned up with fine sandpaper.

1 Make sure a sharp blade is used at all times when cutting thin plywood.

2 Use scissors to cut curves in the plywood. Smooth off rough edges with sandpaper.

## CUTTING IDENTICAL SHAPES

A number of projects call for identical shapes to be cut, such as legs, or the jacket on the climbing monkey. To do this, double-sided tape is used to stick the two pieces of wood together, then the shape is cut out with a fretsaw. The pieces are then separated using a blunt knife. Any damage to the surface caused by the tape is easily sanded away.

1 Stick two pieces of wood together using double-sided tape.

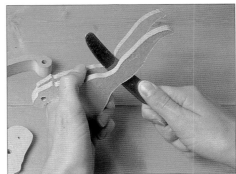

2 Cut out the shape using a fretsaw, then separate the two pieces using a blunt knife.

## CUTTING PERSPEX

Care must be taken when cutting perspex to ensure that the edge does not get damaged. The best way to protect it is to sandwich the perspex between offcuts of MDF held together with double-sided tape. Cut through all three layers with a fretsaw, then carefully separate with a blunt knife taking great care not to scratch the surface.

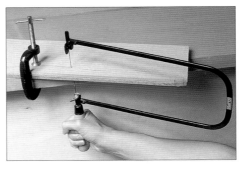

1 The sandwiched perspex is well protected when sawing.

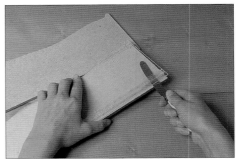

2 Take care not to scratch the perspex when separating it from the MDF.

## SAWING DOWELS

Dowels can be fiddly things to cut, but the job can be made much easier by making this simple home-made dowel vice to steady them. Tack two pieces of flat dowel along a 20cm (8in) length of waste wood, leaving a gap in the middle wide enough to fit in a dowel rod. Use a junior hacksaw to cut the pieces, using the end of the vice as a visual check that the cut is at right angles. Thinner dowels may need wedging in place with a short offcut of dowel.

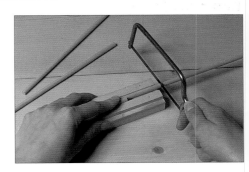

# DRILLING

The main point to watch when drilling is that the item being drilled is held securely to ensure a straight hole is made. With larger pieces this is not so difficult, but small pieces can prove very fiddly. Fortunately simple vices are easy to make to help with this task.

## DRILLING AT RIGHT ANGLES

Unless you have the luxury of a bench drill or a drill stand, drilling at right angles can present problems. A simple aid to accurate drilling can be made by simply screwing two blocks of wood together, making sure the inside of the 'L' is square to the base. The drill is then placed in the inside corner of the 'L' where it is supported and guided straight into the wood.

## DRILLING DOWELS

Dowels have a habit of rolling around as you try to drill them making accurate drilling difficult. This can be remedied by resting the dowel in the same vice used for cutting. Hold the dowel tight into the groove when drilling. For a thin dowel, use an offcut to help wedge it tight in the vice.

## DRILLING AND PLUGGING INTO MDF

Screws and screw eyes used in MDF tend to work loose as the board particles crumble away. To stop this from happening, a piece of dowel needs to be inserted into the MDF to provide firm anchorage for the screw. To do this, drill a hole and glue in a length of dowel just below the point where the screw will enter the MDF. Make a pilot hole for the screw and then twist into position.

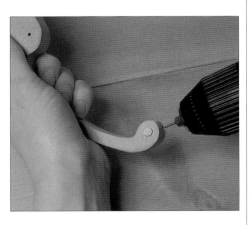

## DRILLING BALLS

Wooden balls are extremely difficult to drill unless they are held steady. This home-made vice is perfect for the job. Drill holes into an offcut of MDF slightly smaller than the balls you want to drill. The ball can then be held steady with a pair of pliers.

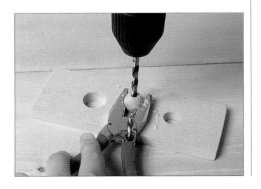

## DRILLING THIN PIECES

Small shapes are also fiddly to drill and again the secret is to find a way of holding them securely in position while drilling. One way to do this is to use a small 'G' clamp to hold several thicknesses of wood together. They will then be steady enough to drill. To make sure the clamp does not damage the pieces, put offcuts between the clamp and the shapes.

# DRILLING TOOLS

The best drilling tool to use is a power drill. It makes any drilling job quick and painless. The changeable drill bits mean you can make whatever size hole is needed from large dowel holes to tiny pilot holes. Alternatively you can use a hand drill.

**Power drill** *Available as cordless or with a cable, most have a variable speed control on the trigger and a chuck that will take the finest of drill bits, making them ideal for use when making toys.*

# MODELLING

If you haven't tried modelling before, then this is your chance. Once you get started, it is surprising how quickly a recognisable shape begins to emerge. Small figures such as the Drinking Cats can be shaped by rolling and pinching the clay or putty. Finer details are then added using a wooden sculptor's tool. If you do not have one of these, improvise by using any similar shaped wooden or plastic implement, such as a lollipop or cocktail stick. For the larger figures, a frame of sculptor's mesh gives a base on which to work up the shape. All these materials you will find in any good art or modelling shop.

## EPOXY PUTTY

Epoxy putty comes in a variety of colours and grades and is a strong and versatile product. It will stick to almost anything, and once dry, can be drilled, sanded, sawn, turned and painted. As with all products, (Milliput Standard is used in the projects), the manufacturer's instructions and safety warnings should be carefully read first.

Epoxy putty is about the consistency of clay and can be modelled using the same tools. When the putty is dry it can be drilled, but on thinner sections it is a good idea to make the holes with a piece of thin wire while the clay is still workable. This stuff sets like rock so make sure tools are cleaned in water as you work.

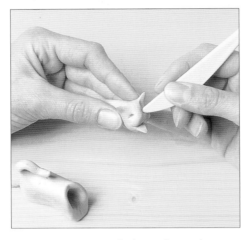

*Use fingers to create the basic shape, then refine using sculpting tools.*

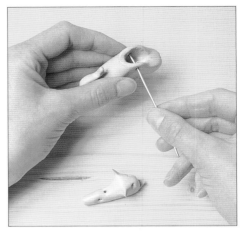

*On a thin part of a shape, make the hole with a piece of wire before the putty sets.*

## AIR DRYING CLAY

When used in conjunction with wire or sculptor's mesh, air drying modelling materials such as DAS, can be used to create quite complex structures. Gradually build up the form by pushing small pieces of clay into the mesh. Do not be tempted to put on large pieces and manipulate them into place as it is much more difficult to create a good shape this way. Use water to keep the clay workable until you have the shape required. If a mistake is made, gently scrape back the clay with a modelling tool and then apply new pieces of clay.

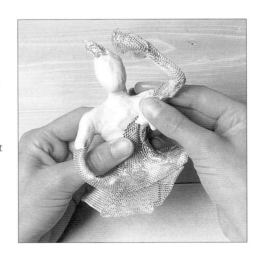

Modelling tools and materials can be found in any good art or modelling shop. The sculptor's mesh and air drying clay are used to make the enchanting Spinning Harlequin (pages 74 – 79).

## SCULPTOR'S MESH

This is used to make a framework of the basic shape. The model is then built up on top in clay. For small figures it is best to cut out and bend one piece of mesh rather than patch together a number of pieces. Work out the shape of the figure and how the mesh needs to be cut to enable the one piece to make up the shape. Mark, then cut out the basic shape with scissors. Carefully and neatly roll and fold the mesh into the form you require.

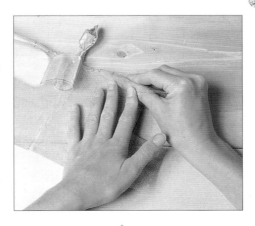

# Papier Mache

## WHITTLING

As with modelling clay, whittle away small pieces at a time. It is important to always work with a sharp knife as this is much safer and also prevents bad cuts being made on the wood. To avoid accidents cut away from your body. When working into a crevice it is sometimes unavoidable to pull the blade towards you. In this instance, use a peeling action which keeps the thumb out of the way, below the line of the blade. Avoid cutting with the grain as the blade will run deep.

Papier mâché is a cheap yet very effective model building material. French for "chewed paper", papier mâché is made by either pulping paper or layering small strips of paper as in the projects in this book. To make the form as strong as possible, the strips are coated in diluted PVA glue to create a tough, lightweight, laminated surface.

To give strength to the papier mâché, it is important to build up several even layers of strips. By using two different colour papers in alternate layers, it is easy to see when one layer is complete before applying the next. When tearing the paper to make the strips, be sure to tear with the paper grain. The paper will easily tear in a straight line down the grain rather than creating jagged, misshapen strips.

Another way of using papier mâché is to cover a cardboard shape in paper strips. For greater strength two or more pieces of card can be stuck together with double-sided tape and the edges joined with masking tape.

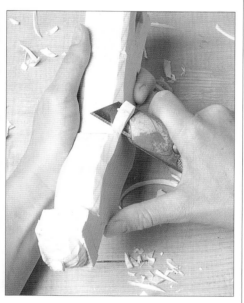

**1** Be sure to tear along the grain of the paper when making the papier mâché strips.

**2** Use a different coloured paper on alternate layers to ensure even coverage.

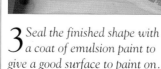

**3** Seal the finished shape with a coat of emulsion paint to give a good surface to paint on.

# DECORATING

Making your toy is only half of the story. Next comes the fun part of decorating. Use the pictures of the projects as a guide when decorating, but feel free to colour your toy exactly as you please. Mark out the pattern lightly in pencil first and when you are happy with the shapes, then start to apply the colour. Do not be afraid to make mistakes, if the worst comes to the worst you can always cover over any accidents with paint or a strip of paper, and start again.

## CRAYONS AND COLOURED PENCILS

Wax crayons and coloured pencils are used to decorate the paper and card projects. They come in a fantastic number of colours, though most of us only have a limited range and tend to use them in flat colour blocks. Interesting textures can be created by drawing over a coloured pencil colour with a contrasting colour wax crayon, then scraping back through the top coat with a hard lead pencil or a craft knife blade.

1 *Colour in the blocks of colour with a pencil. Go over areas with a wax crayon.*

2 *Scrape over the wax with a sharp point to allow the under colour to show through.*

## PAINTING

Paint is used to decorate papier mâché, clay, epoxy putty, wooden, plywood and MDF projects. Water-based paints are used on all the projects as they are easier to handle and cleaner to use than oil paints. Use either acrylic or poster paints. An undercoat of good quality white emulsion paint should be applied before decorating, to give an even coloured background and provide a key for the decoration to bond to. Some colours might need two coats to give a satisfactory finish and for durability all should be finished with an appropriate varnish.

As none of the projects are very large, use small brushes throughout. A small decorating brush can be used to apply the undercoat and any large areas of top colour. Artist's brushes will be needed for detailed work. Always wash brushes out thoroughly when changing from one colour to the next, and after use.

### SOLID COLOUR

Outline the area to be painted with a faint pencil line. Apply the paint in even strokes, taking care not to create drips and dribbles. If a second coat is needed, wait until the first is thoroughly dry before applying the final coat.

### HIGHLIGHTS AND SHADING

Areas of light and shade are created on the figure being decorated to give it form. Highlights are added by applying white or a similar light colour where the light would hit the toy. Likewise, areas of shadow are made darker, thus giving a more three dimensional look to the figure.

### COLOURWASHING

A colourwash is created by thinning a water-based paint with water to give a soft colouring which will bring out the grain of the wood. For this reason it is particularly good for adding form to simple carved figures. Start by painting the figure with a coat of diluted paint, and while still wet, flood in thicker paint to areas which need to be darker. To create highlights, lift off some of the colour with a piece of rag or a clean brush.

# TEMPLATES

## MASKING

Masking tape can be used to give sharp, straight edges or simple designs. Stick the tape over the area to be left blank, paint over the top of it and once dry, peel back the tape and retouch any colour that has seeped under the tape.

## TEXTURE GEL AND PASTE

Beaded texture gel is a thick whitish paste designed to create textures in acrylic paint. It can be applied with a stencil brush, palette knife or paintbrush depending on the effect you require. Similar effects can be created by mixing sand with PVA glue.

## RELIEF LINER

Relief liner is used mainly by glass painters as an outliner. It comes in gold, silver and black and is available in art shops. The liner comes in a tube with a nozzle attached and is applied by holding the tube like a pen and gently squeezing it as you guide the liner around the outline. It leaves a raised bead of colour that adheres well to most surfaces.

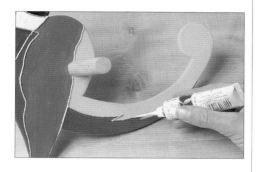

## APPLIED DECORATION

Small packs of pre-cut stick-on paper shapes are widely available in stationers, craft and art shops and can be a useful source of decorative motives. Some toys move at high speed so any applied decoration should be glued and varnished into position.

## COLLAGE

Collage is the art of building up a picture with pieces of paper, fabric or other materials. Use PVA glue which is transparent when dry to stick fabric or paper to toys. When dry, finish with a coat of varnish to protect the surface.

The trace-off shapes for making templates for a number of the projects are given at the back of the book. To make a template, simply trace the given shape onto tracing paper using a pencil. Turn over the paper and go over the outline again. Turn the paper back and place on thin card. Trace over the outline with the pencil onto the card, making sure any drill holes are clearly marked. Cut out the shape carefully with a sharp pair of scissors.

To use the template, hold it down firmly on the material to be cut to shape. Draw around the template with a sharp pencil. Cut out around the outline.

*Trace the outline from the back of the book onto card. Carefully cut out the shape to create the template. Hold the card template firmly down on the material to be shaped, and draw the outline with a pencil.*

# Button Buzzer

## IN CARD AND STRING

Called a buzzer because of the noise it makes, this toy can be as simple as a button on a loop of string, or as elaborate as you like. Here, bright ribbons and beads create a Catherine wheel of colour, while opposite are a host of other buzzer ideas.

## TOOLS & MATERIALS

- Thick card, 9cm (3½in) square
- Large button
- Ribbon, 1.5m (1⅝yd)
- Coloured beads
- String or cord, 1m (1⅛yd)
- Pencil
- Felt tip pens
- Fine sandpaper
- Double-sided tape
- PVA glue
- Compass
- Scissors
- Bradawl

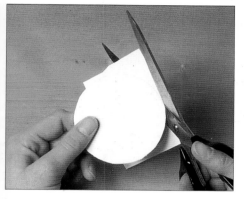

1 Draw an 8cm (3⅛in) diameter circle onto the card using a compass. Cut out the circle and lightly sand the edges.

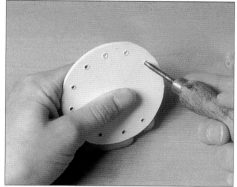

2 Divide the circle into twelve equal parts. With the compass at the circle setting, place the point and pencil on the circumference. Mark where the pencil touches. Move compass point to this mark. Repeat around the circle. Move compass point to the centre of two marks and repeat the process. Mark 8mm (⁵⁄₁₆in) in from each point and pierce with a bradawl.

3 Lightly sand away any rough bits. Colour both sides of the disc with a felt tip pen, and use double-sided tape to stick a button to the centre. Pierce through two of the button's holes with a bradawl.

4 Cut twelve lengths of ribbon roughly 10cm (4in) long and thread them with coloured beads. Push one end of each ribbon strip through one of the twelve outer holes and secure with a knot. Seal the ends of the ribbon with a small dab of PVA glue. Allow to dry.

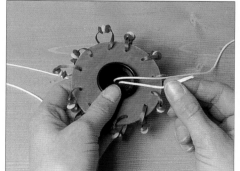

5 Thread the two loose ends of the string through the button holes and tie together with a knot. The buzzer is now complete and ready to spin. Hold the loops, one in each hand and swing the spinner over and over to twist the string. Keep the wheel in motion by gently pulling apart and releasing the tension.

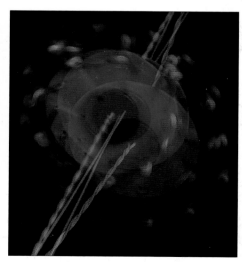

# GALLOPING CAROUSEL

## IN CARD AND PAPIER MACHE

EASY

The animals on this colourful carousel are inexpensive Christmas tree decorations. They can be set to gallop around and around on this fairground carousel made from a few simple materials. If you are feeling adventurous, try making your own animals, following the Traditional Carousel instructions.

### TOOLS & MATERIALS

- Two sheets of card 25cm (10in) square
- Large button
- Thin nylon cord or string, 1m (1⅛yd)
- Paper plate approx 24cm (9½in) diameter
- Newspaper, two different colours
- Cardboard tube, 15cm (6in) long
- PVA glue
- Christmas tree animals
- Coloured ribbons
- Double-sided tape
- Masking tape
- White emulsion paint
- Water-based paints
- Gold and silver relief liner
- Acrylic varnish
- Compass, pencil
- Sharp scissors
- Stapler
- Bradawl
- Thin wire
- Small decorating brush
- Artist's brush

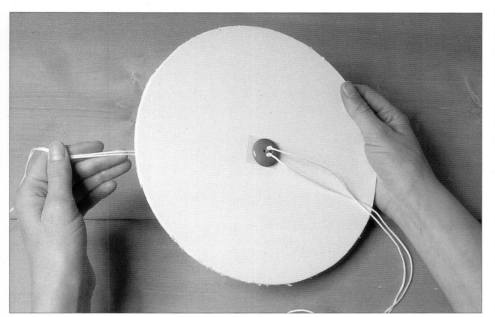

1 Stick the two sheets of card together with double-sided tape. Draw a 24cm (9½in) diameter circle on one side. Cut out the circle. Stick a large button to the centre of the circle with double-sided tape. Make holes through two of the button's holes using a bradawl. Divide the nylon cord into three equal lengths and mark the lengths with two knots. Thread the two ends through the buttonholes and card.

2 Find the centre of the paper plate with the compass, and draw and cut out a small circle. Cut straight from the edge of the plate into the centre, turn the plate upside down and overlap the cut edges to form a dome. Staple the overlapping edges together. Pass the string ends through the hole and staple the dome to the card circle. Cover the overlapping edges with tape. Tie the threaded ends of the string together to form a loop.

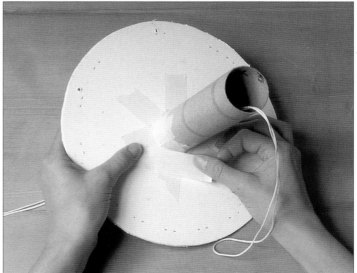

3 Tape the cardboard tube to the flat underside of the canopy, using masking tape, so that it covers the button. Make sure the cardboard tube is at right angles to the card.

4 Tear the newspaper into strips roughly 2.5 x 10cm (1 x 4in). Cover the dome with one layer of strips coated with PVA diluted 50 per cent with water. Smooth the strips down with a decorating brush. Make sure the strips overlap and cover the rim.

5 Turn the carousel over and cover the flat underside and the cardboard tube with overlapping pasted paper strips. When the first layer is complete, strengthen the papier mâché with a second covering applied at right angles to the first. Use a different coloured paper for each layer to distinguish one layer from the next. Leave to dry.

6 When the carousel is thoroughly dry, push the string inside to keep it clean, and apply an undercoat of white emulsion paint. Allow the paint to dry, then gently sand away any rough edges.

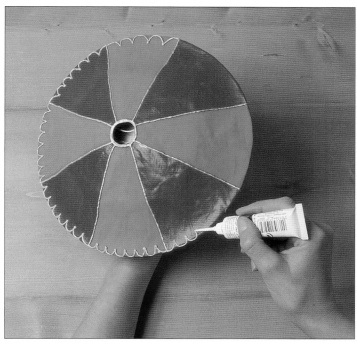

7 Mark out a decorative design in pencil, and paint using an artists brush, with strong flat colours. Keep the design and colours simple and fresh. Give the paint plenty of time to dry before applying other colours on top to prevent one running into the other.

8 Cover any ragged edges in the painting with a fine bead of relief liner and add scallops and dots round the canopy edge. Decorate the centre column in the same way and hang up to dry. Finish with a coat of acrylic varnish.

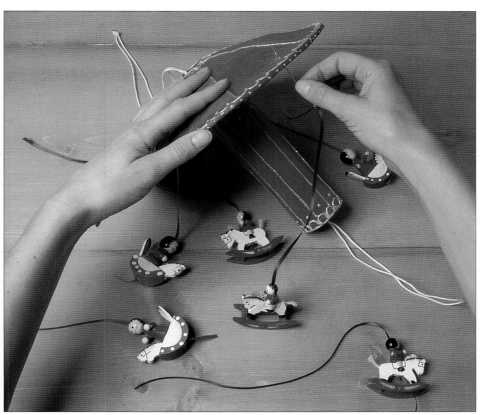

9 Use a bradawl to make holes through the canopy to attach the animals. Wrap a piece of thin wire round the ribbon end and thread it through the holes. Make sure the carousel is balanced before finally tying the animals on and sealing the knots with a spot of glue.

# TRADITIONAL CAROUSEL

## IN PLYWOOD AND MDF

HARD

The graceful movement of this toy is based on the motion of a maypole – remove the canopy, and replace the horses with children and that is what you would have. Balance is all-important to the carousel's smooth action and although it requires a higher level of skill and patience than the previous toy, it is actually not very difficult to make.

## TOOLS & MATERIALS

- 19mm (¾in) MDF, 18cm (7⅛in) square
- 16mm (⅝in) dowel rod, 26cm (10¼in) long
- 6mm (¼in) MDF, 26cm (10¼in) square
- 12mm (½in) MDF, 26cm (10¼in) square
- 12mm (½in) MDF, 16 x 32cm (6¼ x12 ⅝in)
- Six 6mm (¼in) dowel rod, 20cm (8in) long
- 1.5mm (¹⁄₁₆in) plywood, 80 x 10cm (32 x 4in)
- Six 19mm (¾in) wooden balls
- Small wooden knob
- Eight small metal eyelets
- Thin card and tracing paper
- Coloured ribbon
- Panel pins
- Emulsion paint
- Acrylic paint
- Gold relief liner
- Acrylic satin varnish
- Jigsaw
- Fretsaw
- Drill
- Drill bits: same size as dowels plus 19mm (¾in) and fine
- Clamp
- Sandpaper
- Double-sided tape
- PVA glue
- Compass
- Pencil
- Set square and ruler
- Bulldog clip
- Small decorating brush
- Artist's brush

**1** Locate the centre of the 19mm (¾in) MDF piece by drawing two diagonal lines from corner to corner. The centre is where the lines intersect. Place the compass point in the centre and draw a 15cm (6in) circle. Cut out with a jigsaw. Drill a 16mm (⅝in) hole in the centre of the circle and glue in the 26cm (10¼in) length of 16mm (⅝in) dowel. Use a drill stand or a home-made drill jig to ensure the pole is upright as this is essential for the toy to work.

**2** Draw diagonals to find the centre of the thinner 26cm (10¼in) MDF square and using the compass, draw a 23cm (9in) circle. Divide the circumference into six equal pieces, marked by slightly curving pencil lines. Reduce the compass setting by 16mm (⅝in) and mark where the lines cross. These are the drill hole positions for the uprights. Stick the two 26cm (10¼in) squares together using double-sided tape.

**3** Drill a fine hole through the centre of the 26cm (10¼in) square to mark it on the underside. Drill six, 6mm (¼in) holes to take the uprights and cut out the circle with a jigsaw.

4 Sand the edges to even up the shape and remove any rough bits. Clearly mark joining positions across the edges of the two pieces as they must go back in the same position later, and separate the discs.

5 Set the compass to 9cm (3½in) and draw an inner circle on the 6mm (¼in) disc. Drill a pilot hole large enough for the jigsaw blade and remove the inner circle.

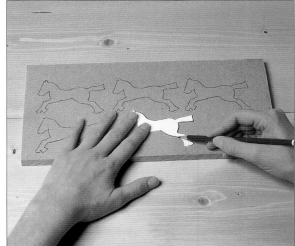

6 To find the four hang points, rule a line through the centre of the 12mm (½in) disc and with a set square mark a line, again through the centre at right-angles to the first. Set a compass to 5cm (2in) and tick where it crosses the lines. Drill four pilot holes for the eyelets and a 19mm (¾in) hole in the centre for the pole to go through.

7 Make a horse template using the trace-off motif on page 118. Using this template, draw six horses onto the 12mm (½in) MDF.

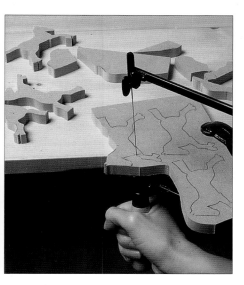

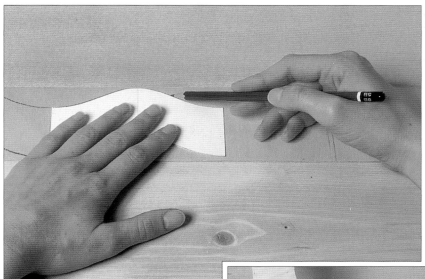

8 Cut out the horses with a fretsaw. To make accurate cutting easier, clamp the workpiece to the table.

9 Mark and drill through the horses' backs with a 6mm (¼in) drill. Clamp two or three together to make it easier to hold them still. Cut six 20cm (8in) lengths of 6mm (¼in) dowel. Tap the rods through the horses, half 6cm (2⅜in) from the base to the saddle, the others, 10cm (4in) from the base to saddle. Glue and leave to dry.

10 Drill half way through the wooden balls with a 6mm (¼in) drill. Use a block of wood with a drilled hole to rest the balls in and a pair of pliers to keep them still while drilling.

11 For the canopy, roll the top disc along the plywood to establish the canopy length. Make a canopy template using the trace-off motif on page 118. Draw the wavy shape with the template and cut out using the fretsaw, leaving a 19mm (¾in) overlap in case of errors. Smooth off with fine sandpaper.

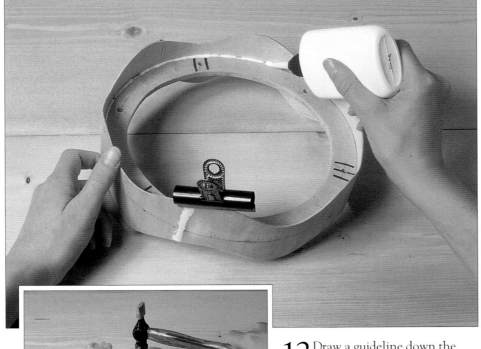

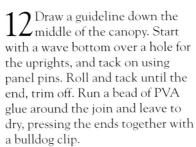

**12** Draw a guideline down the middle of the canopy. Start with a wave bottom over a hole for the uprights, and tack on using panel pins. Roll and tack until the end, trim off. Run a bead of PVA glue around the join and leave to dry, pressing the ends together with a bulldog clip.

**13** Paint the horses with one coat of white emulsion. Add a small amount of emerald green acrylic paint to the white to paint the rest of the carousel pieces.

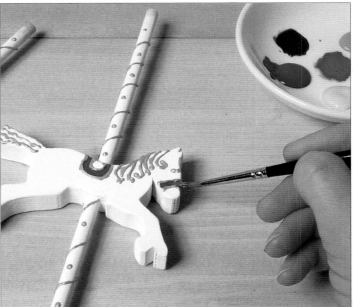

**14** Draw the mane and harness onto the horses using gold relief. Decorate the poles by gently turning them as you apply the gold. If the gold runs unevenly, clean the nozzle end and leave to settle.

**15** Paint in the saddle and harness with the bright acrylic paint, using a different colour for each horse.

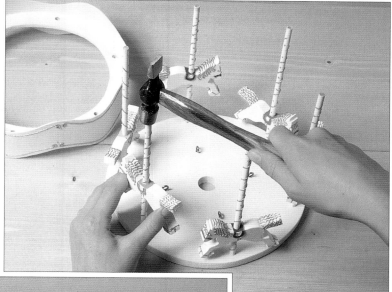

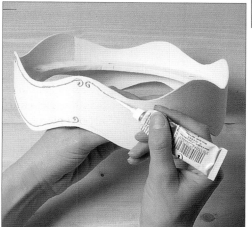

**16** Trail gold round the canopy edge following the contours. Screw the eyelets into the baseplate. Glue and tap the horse poles into their baseplate holes. Ease the canopy holes onto the poles using the original marks to align them. Tap the canopy down 19mm (¾in) and glue in position.

**17** Push the balls onto the top of the poles. Retouch any damage and decorate the balls with gold paint and the same colour paint as the horse under them. Varnish the whole carousel with acrylic satin finish varnish.

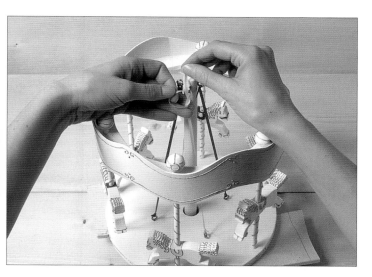

**18** Drill four pilot holes 1cm (⅜in) down from the top of the centre pole. Lower the carousel over the pole and screw in the eyelets. Tie the ribbons to the bottom eyelets. Put offcuts of MDF of the same thickness between the two bases as temporary spacers and tie off the ribbons at the top. Remove the spacers and check the movement. If it runs freely, seal the knots with glue and finish the pole with the decorated knob.

# ZOETROPE

## IN PLYWOOD

The zoetrope was invented in 1869 at the dawn of moving images. This remarkably simple device was greeted with awe, and became known as the "wheel of life". You can make your own moving story following the instructions below.

**1** Make templates for the slots and scallops, and handle winder from the trace-offs on page 118. Use the template to mark the scallops and slots onto the thin plywood. Make sure the slots are lined up straight. The ends will not be identical as there is a 19mm (¾in) overlap.

**2** Cut out the slots with a sharp craft knife, using a metal ruler to guide the blade. Replace the blade as soon as it begins to blunt.

## TOOLS & MATERIALS

- Thin card and tracing paper
- 1.5mm (1/16in) plywood, 66 x 18cm (26 x 7⅛in)
- 12mm (½in) plywood, 25cm (10in) square
- 2.2cm (⅞in) copper plumbing pipe, 12cm (4¾in) long
- 16mm (⅝in) dowel, 16cm (6¼in) long
- 6mm (¼in) dowel, 19mm (¾in) long
- Small wooden knob
- Metallic gilding wax
- Pencil

- Sandpaper
- Glue
- Panel pins
- Scissors
- Sharp craft knife
- Metal ruler
- Compass
- Drill
- Drill bits: same sizes as dowels
- Clamp or vice
- Fretsaw or jigsaw
- Pin hammer
- Masking tape

**ANIMATION STRIPS**
- Thin card, 65 x 5cm (25⅝ x 2in)
- Coloured pencils
- Paints and brushes

*The animation strips are made from thin card cut to 65 x 5cm (25⅝in x 2in) and decorated with an image sequence which appears to move when the toy is turned. Draw, paint or stick the images onto the card, then slide the strip down below the slots, hold the copper tube in one hand and wind the handle.*

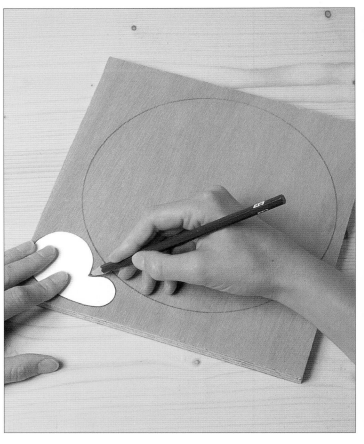

3 Cut the scallops around the base with a sharp pair of scissors or a craft knife. Round off any jagged edges with fine sandpaper.

4 Draw a 20cm (8in) circle on the 12mm (½in) plywood square with the compass. Draw around the winding handle template onto a corner of the plywood, not too close to the circle.

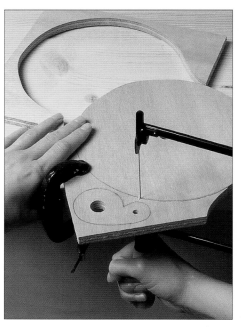

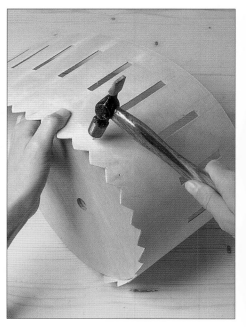

5 Drill a hole the same size as the thicker dowel in the centre of the circle, and one into the winder. Use a drill stand or a home-made jig to ensure the drill holes are at right-angles. Drill a 6mm (¼in) hole in the winder where the knob attaches.

6 Secure the work to a bench and cut out both shapes using a fretsaw or jigsaw. Any mistakes will be hidden by the skirt or can be filled with wood filler.

7 Draw a guide line on the inside of the skirt just above the scallops. Roll the skirt round the base, gluing and pinning in place as you go.

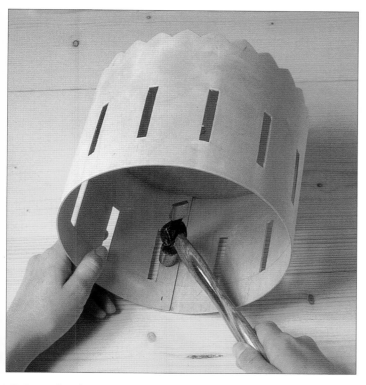

8 Run a bead of glue down the overlap and secure with panel pins. Bend the pins over to lie flat on the inside of the drum.

9 Glue the small dowel into the winder. Drill a 6mm (¼in) hole in the back of the knob, dab glue into the hole and push the knob onto the dowel protruding from the winder. Gently tap down with a hammer if necessary. Wipe off any excess glue from the winder.

10 Glue the thicker dowel into the handle, slip the copper pipe over the dowel and glue into the base. Allow the glue to dry and clean the whole toy with fine sandpaper.

11 Run a length of masking tape round the top of the skirt about 12mm (½in) from the edge, and another just at the top of the scallops. Colour the scallops and exposed strip with metallic gilding wax. Leave the wax to soak in for a few minutes, buff with a soft cloth, then peel off the masking tape.

# SPINNING PARROT 1

## IN CARD

The spinning motion of this exotic parrot is achieved in the same way as the traditional yo-yo. This movement will work equally well with any cut-out bird or animal, so you could end up with a whole menagerie of spinning creatures.

EASY

### TOOLS & MATERIALS

- Tracing paper
- Thick plain white card 30 x 25cm (12 x 10in)
- String or ribbon 2m (2¼yd)
- Hexagonal pencil
- Coloured pencils
- Wax crayons
- Sticky tape
- Scissors
- Craft knife (optional)

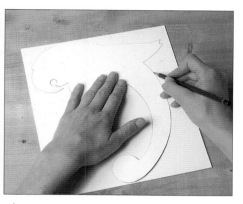

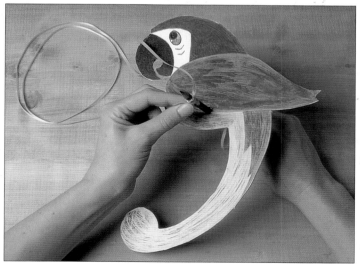

**1** Trace the parrot outline on page 119 onto the thick card to give the parrot's silhouette, and roughly mark the point of balance. Lightly pencil in features like the wing, face and tail feathers. Begin to block in the main colours with coloured pencils. There are hundreds of different coloured parrots so use whatever colours you like.

**2** To create the texture of feathers, colour over the pencil colour with wax crayons, then scrape back to the base colour with a sharp pencil or a craft knife. This gives a three dimensional effect.

**3** When the one side is decorated, cut out the parrot with a pair of sharp scissors. Turn it over and decorate the other side with the same or different colours if wished.

**4** Push a hexagonal pencil (round ones slip) through the centre hole and tape the ribbon to each end. Find the centre of the ribbon and tie a loop. Hang the parrot up and spin it gently round its perch, or put your finger through the loop and use it like a yo-yo.

# SPINNING PARROT 2

## IN PLYWOOD OR MDF

INTERMEDIATE

If you've tried the spinning parrot in card, why not try this one? It will stand harsher treatment and the paint will look brighter on wood, especially if varnished.

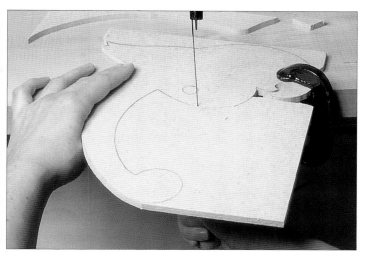

**1** Make a card template from the trace-off on page 119. Draw around the template onto the 6mm (¼in) board. Be sure to mark the perch hole, which is at the point of balance. Put on the protective mask and cut around the outline with a jigsaw or fretsaw.

**2** Drill the perch hole, the same size as the perch dowel. Use a drill stand or a home-made jig to ensure the holes are drilled at right angles. Drill holes about 1cm (⅜in) from each end of the perch dowel large enough to take the ribbon.

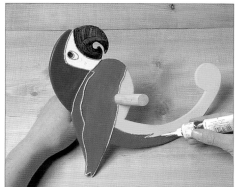

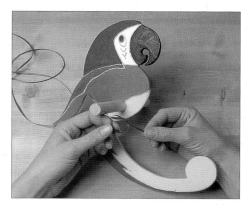

**3** Clean around all the outside edges of the parrot with fine sandpaper. Push the perch dowel through the perch hole and centre the parrot on it. Set the parrot at the angle he looks best in relation to the vertical ribbon holes. Glue in position and leave until the glue is set.

**4** Prime the parrot with a coat of white emulsion paint and leave to dry. Pencil in the wings and main features, then paint these areas boldly with artist's brushes, using strong colours. Separate each colour shape with a line of silver colour trail and leave to dry. Finish with a coat of varnish.

**5** Tie a small loop at the centre of the ribbon then thread the ends through the perch holes. Secure the ribbon with a knot large enough to prevent it slipping back through the hole and hang the parrot up to spin. The longer the ribbon the faster it will spin, but don't make it too long.

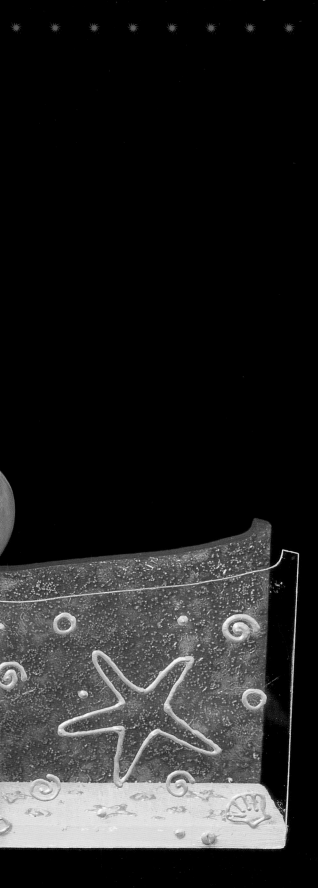

# Swimming Dolphins

## IN WOOD AND PERSPEX

Dolphins are among the best loved creatures living in our seas. A toy could never recreate the true beauty of these sleek playful creatures of the deep, but it can bring a splash of their colour and fun into our lives.

## TOOLS & MATERIALS

- Thin card and tracing paper
- Two pieces 8mm (⁵⁄₁₆in) MDF, 40 x 12cm (15¾ x 4¾in)
- 8mm (⁵⁄₁₆in) softwood, 40 x 6cm (15¾ x 2⅜in)
- Perspex sheet, 40 x 12cm (15¾ x 4¾in)
- 6mm (¼in) MDF, 20cm (8in) square
- 8mm (⁵⁄₁₆in) dowel, 10cm (4in) long

- Two small wooden balls
- Glue
- White emulsion paint
- Acrylic paint
- Stencil cream
- Beaded texture gel
- Gold relief liner
- Gloss acrylic varnish
- Protective mask and goggles

- Double-sided tape
- Pencil
- Round ended knife
- Selection of brushes
- Fretsaw
- Drill
- Drill bits: same size as dowel, and fine
- Pliers
- Clamp
- Small screws

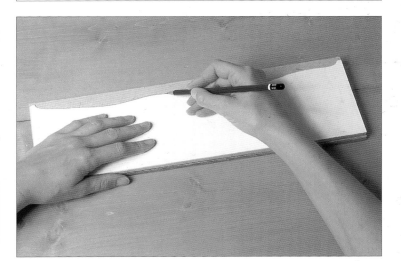

**1** Use double-sided tape to stick together the two pieces of MDF with the sheet of perspex sandwiched between. Make templates from the wave and dolphin trace-offs on pages 120 – 121. Line the wave template up with the edges of the MDF and perspex block and draw around it.

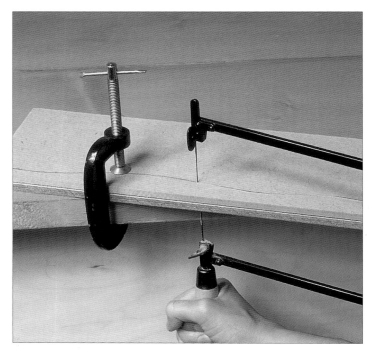

2 Clamp the wood to a solid surface and cut along the pencil line using a fretsaw.

3 Separate the three pieces by sliding a round ended knife carefully between the surfaces and gently prising apart. Take care not to scratch the perspex. Discard one sheet of MDF.

4 Draw around the dolphin template onto the 20cm (8in) square of MDF. Put on the mask and goggles, clamp the dolphin to a solid surface and saw along the pencil lines. Drill a hole between fin and tail to give the fretsaw access to cutting out the inner shape.

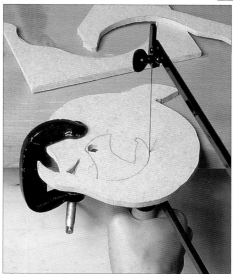

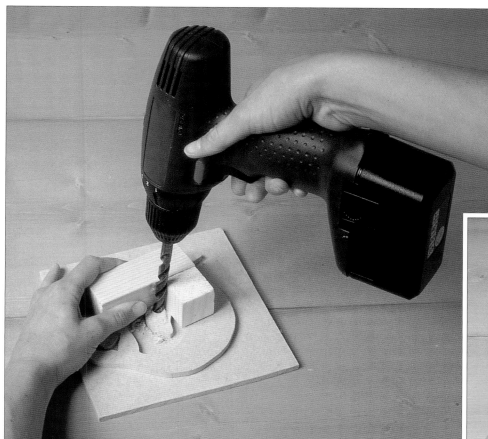

5 Drill a hole to match the dowel width through the fin of the dolphin. Sand all surfaces to prepare for paint and round off any pointed edges. Push the 10cm (4in) length of dowel through the fin, centre the dolphin and glue in position. Paint the dolphin, base and backplate with white emulsion. Leave to dry.

6 Choose a palette of blue acrylic paints and build up colour on the dolphin. Begin with lighter shades and gradually introduce more dense colour using darker blues and greys.

**7** Leave some areas white, and complement with lighter shades of blue and yellow to give form to the dolphin. Highlight the fins and nose with a splash of white paint. Leave to dry, then varnish.

**8** Use beaded texture gel, mixed with blue acrylic paint to colour the backplate, and yellow for the base. Apply with a stencil brush, using a stabbing motion. Similar textures can be created by adding sand and PVA glue to the paint. Leave to dry thoroughly, then varnish the base.

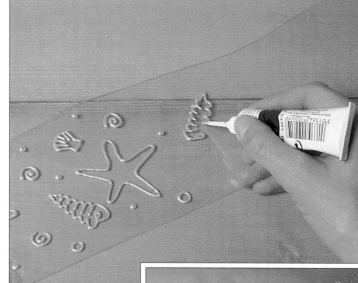

**9** Rub a light blue stencil cream lightly over the blue backboard with your fingertips, the texture will be exaggerated by the contrast in colours. Leave to dry then varnish.

**10** Use a gold relief liner to decorate the perspex and base with simple shapes such as starfish and shells. Leave to dry.

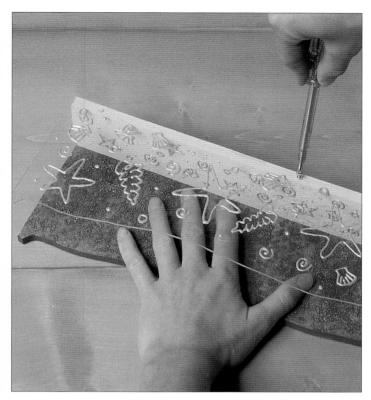

**11** Drill pilot holes through the backplate into the base and glue and screw together. Align the perspex front and drill three pilot holes through into the base, countersink using the 8mm (5⁄16in) drill bit. Screw the two pieces together and cover the screw heads with relief liner.

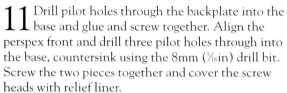

**12** Drill halfway through the two wooden balls using an 8mm (5⁄16in) drill. Hold the balls steady with a home-made ball vice (see page 11). Glue the balls onto either end of the dowel. Your dolphin is ready to rock and roll.

# ROCKING CLOWN

## IN PAPIER MACHE

INTERMEDIATE

This handsome clown refuses to lie down – knock him over and he just sits back up. Made from the simplest of materials, you will need more patience than skill to make him, as it is important to allow plenty of time for drying between each stage. The outcome is, however, well worth the wait.

### TOOLS & MATERIALS

- Large balloon
- String
- Masking tape
- Newspapers, in two colours
- PVA glue
- Petroleum jelly
- White emulsion paint
- Acrylic paints
- Acrylic varnish
- Wool
- Medium grade sandpaper
- Pencil
- Scissors or knife
- Pebble or weight
- Paint brushes

1 Blow up the balloon, hold for twenty seconds then deflate. Repeat twice to stretch the balloon. Blow up the balloon to about ¼ of its full size and tie off. Twist the balloon in two, making a smaller ball for the head. Tie string around the twist and strengthen with masking tape.

2 Tear the newspapers into strips about 2.5 x 10cm (1 x 4in). Dilute the PVA with ⅓ water. Cover the balloon with petroleum jelly and begin applying the strips of newspaper. Drag each strip through the solution of PVA and smooth onto the surface with finger tips.

3 Continue covering, paying particular attention to the neck. Apply eight to ten layers. To ensure even layers, use two different coloured papers on alternate layers so that you can see when a layer is complete. Allow at least twenty-four hours to dry.

4 Draw a line around the clown at about waist height, then make three or four marks at right angles around the line as guide lines to fit the body back together. Cut around the waist line with a knife or a pair of scissors and remove the balloon.

**5** Hold the weight or pebble firmly in place inside the base using masking tape. The weight will create the rocking motion and must be firmly attached. Layer over the masking tape with papier mâché. Do three to four layers then allow about four hours to dry.

**6** Tape the two halves back together, matching up the guide lines carefully. Cover the join with masking tape and repair with three or four layers of papier mâché. Allow to dry.

**7** Smooth any rough edges using medium grade sandpaper and prime with a coat of white emulsion.

**8** Draw the clown's face, arms, and clothing in pencil on both sides of the shape. You can treat each side differently by drawing a happy face on one side and a sad face on the other.

**9** Work with one colour at a time and build up areas of flat colour. If you want to use strong, deep colours you will need to apply two coats of paint. Any mistakes can just be painted over with emulsion to allow you to start again.

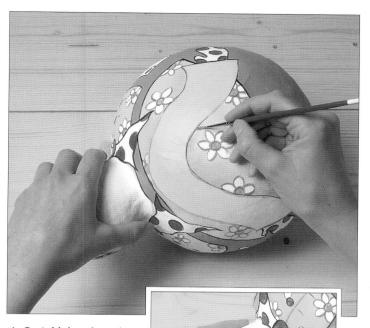

**10** Add details and outlines using a fine brush and paint, or a permanent felt tip marker. Once the decoration is complete, varnish the clown using a clear gloss varnish.

**11** Wrap several layers of wool around a piece of card approximately 15cms (6in) long. Remove the card, tie a length of wool around the centre of the bunch and cut the ends to form a tassel.

**12** Make enough tassels to fit around each side of the clown's head. Glue into position and trim.

# CLOWN AND BUTTERFLY

## IN PAPIER MACHE

This illusion has been used for years by circus clowns, every slight movement of the head travels down the wire and is magnified making the butterfly flutter around your head, just out of reach.

### TOOLS & MATERIALS

- Balloon
- Newspaper, two different colours
- Petroleum jelly
- PVA glue
- Copper wire, 1.3m (1⅜yd)
- Coloured paper
- Tracing paper
- Stickers
- White emulsion
- Acrylic paint
- Pen and pencil
- Acrylic gloss varnish
- Small wooden ball or bead
- Wool
- Masking tape
- Double-sided tape
- Scissors
- Bradawl
- Small drill
- Artist's brushes

**1** Blow up the balloon to roughly the size of your head. Tear the newspaper into strips and squares. Cover the balloon with petroleum jelly and build up alternate coloured layers of strips over half the balloon. Drag each strip through a solution of PVA diluted with ⅓ water and mould to the surface with finger tips. Build up eight to ten layers. Allow twenty-four hours to dry.

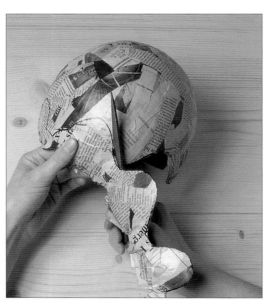

**2** Draw onto the papier mâché the shape of the clown's brow line, around the ears and down the back of his hairline. Pop the balloon and cut along these lines with a pair of scissors.

**3** Cut a 1.3m (1⅜yd) length of soft wire and wrap it around the head, leaving one end of the wire long and the other short. Twist the two ends together at the front between the brow shapes and secure with masking tape. Continue taping until the wire is covered.

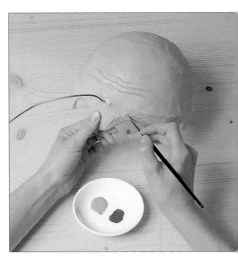

4 Papier mâché four layers over the tape to cover it, and over the rim of the hat to create a smooth edge.

5 Once the hat is completely dry, seal it inside and out by painting with white emulsion. Allow to dry.

6 Paint the outer surface using a flesh coloured acrylic paint. Add some furrows in his brow and paint on eyebrows using a small paintbrush. Finish with two coats of acrylic gloss varnish.

7 Wind brightly coloured wool around a piece of card 25cm (10in) long. Remove the card and tie a piece of wool around the centre to form a tassel. Trim the tassel ends. Wrap a small piece of masking tape around each end of the strand of wool tying the tassel, to make the ends easier to thread.

8 Mark with a pencil an even number of holes around the sides and back of the head, to tie in the hair. Each hair tassel needs two holes, one 16mm (⅝in) above the other. Poke each hole through using a bradawl.

9 Thread one taped tassel end into a lower hole and the other through the hole directly above it. Tie the two ends together on the inside. Repeat with each tassel until the head is covered. Tidy the inside by tying any loose ends together, and cutting off any excess wool.

10 To make the butterfly, fold the coloured paper in half and trace off the shape on page 119. Cut out the shape and open out the butterfly. Decorate with coloured stickers or pens.

11 Drill a hole the same gauge as the wire, half way through the small wooden ball. Glue onto the end of the wire to make it safe. Attach the butterfly to the wire using double-sided sticky tape, and bend the wire so that the butterfly is just out of reach when the cap is worn. Now try to catch it.

# JUGGLING THUDS

## BALLONS AND RICE

EASY

Most people think of balls, hoops or clubs when they hear the word juggling. These simple rice-filled balloons are in fact ideal for all juggling movements especially when you are learning, as they stay exactly where you drop them!

### TOOLS & MATERIALS

To make three thuds:
- Six good quality brightly coloured balloons
- Two cups uncooked rice
- Sharp scissors

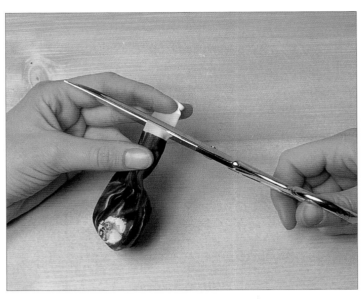

**1** Blow up a balloon and hold it for twenty seconds to stretch it, then let it down. Repeat this with all the balloons then turn them inside out to dry. Turn them back the right way and cut about half the neck off the three less colourful ones.

**2** Push the rice firmly into the cut balloons with your fingers. Fill the balloons until each fits snugly into the palm of your hand.

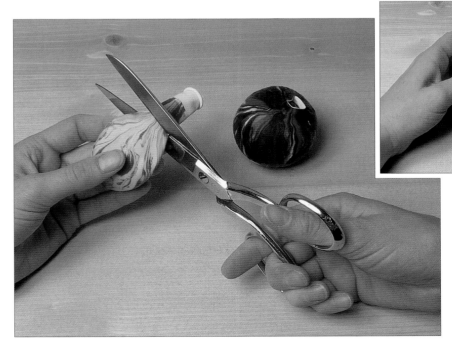

**3** Cut the necks off the remaining balloons. Stretch over the open end of each thud, covering as much of its surface as possible.

# HOW TO JUGGLE THREE BALLS

Before you begin to juggle with three balls, first practise holding them in your hands. Throw the third ball from hand to hand, holding the other two while you do so. When you feel comfortable holding, throwing, and catching all three you are ready to move on and learn the three ball cascade.

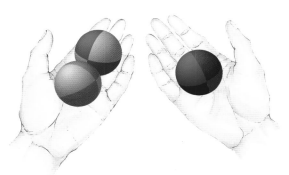

**1** Hold two juggling balls in your left hand and the third ball in your right.

**2** Throw the first ball from your left hand up into the air.

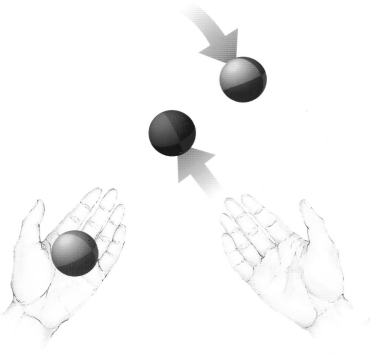

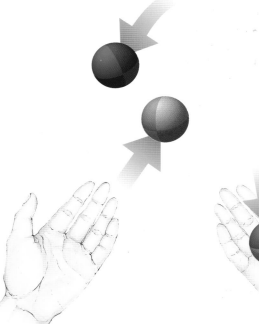

**3** As it reaches the high point of its trajectory, throw up the ball from your right hand.

**4** Catch the first ball in your right hand and as the second ball reaches its highest point, throw the remaining ball from your left hand. Continue in this way.

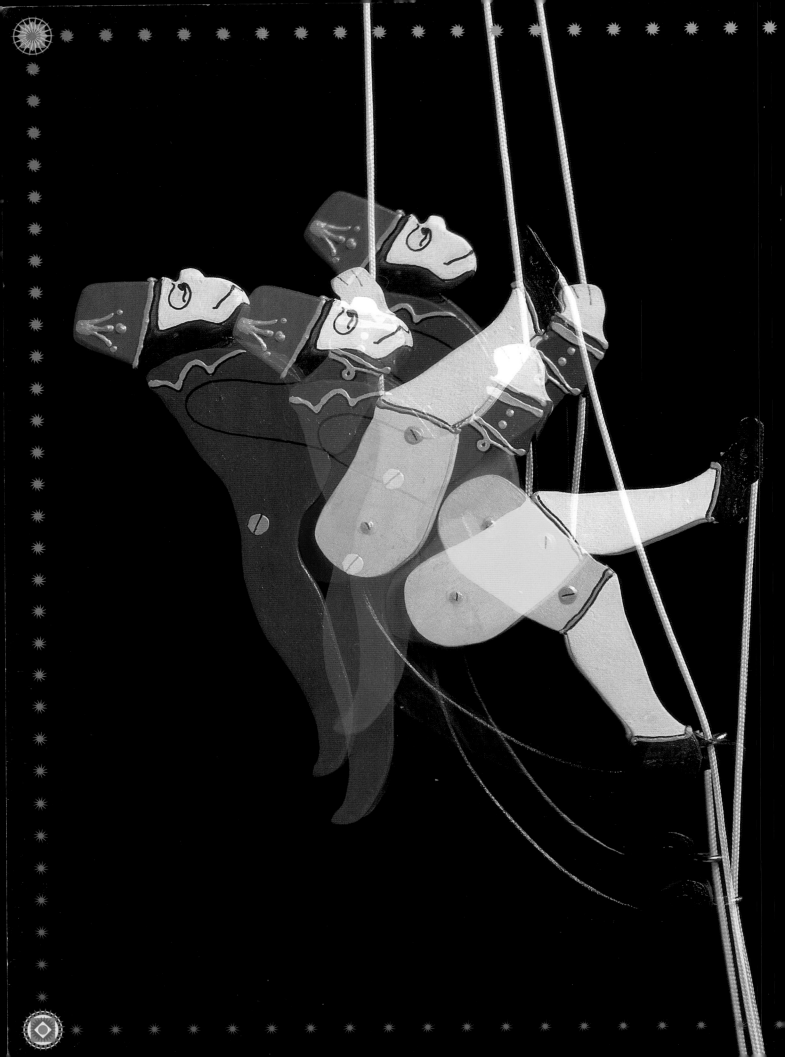

# CLIMBING MONKEY

## IN MDF

There is a long tradition of dressed monkey toys and automata, from smoking monkeys in the 1860s through to the clockwork pressed tin German toys of the 1950s. This monkey climbs when you pull and release the cord and is a great favourite with children and grown-ups alike.

### TOOLS & MATERIALS

- Thin card and tracing paper
- Two pieces 6mm (¼in) MDF, 18 x 10cm (7⅛ x 4in)
- 19mm (¾in) MDF, 25 x 10cm (10 x 4in)
- 6mm (¼in) dowel, 10cm (4in) long
- Coathanger wire or similar, 10cm (4in) long
- Nylon cord, 1.5m (1⅝yd)
- Round shearing elastic, 30cm (12in)
- 2 small screw eyes
- 2 short panel pins
- Wooden ball
- Wood filler
- Sandpaper
- Glue
- Double-sided tape
- White primer paint
- Acrylic paints
- Colour trailer
- Marker pen and pencil
- Acrylic varnish
- Protective mask and goggles
- Fretsaw and/or jigsaw
- Drill
- Drill bits: to match dowel, and fine
- Pin hammer
- Long nosed pliers

**1** Stick the two pieces of 6mm (¼in) MDF together with double-sided sticky tape. Make templates of the monkey's body, legs and jacket from the trace-offs on page 122.

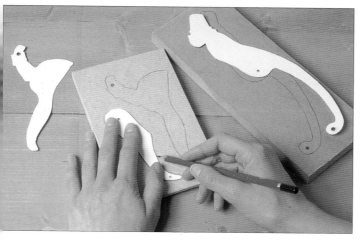

**2** Draw around the templates to mark out the jacket and legs onto the joined 6mm (¼in) pieces. Draw the body onto the 18mm (¾in) piece. Be sure to mark the drill hole positions.

**3** Drill three 6mm (¼in) holes for the dowels: one in the monkey's tail, one near the top of the leg, and one in his hands. Using a drill bit the same gauge as the wire, drill three holes in the leg section, and a slightly larger hole at the hip joint on the body section. Use a drill stand or a small home-made jig to ensure the holes are drilled at right angles.

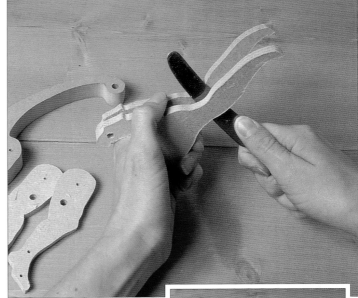

**4** Put on the mask and goggles. Cut out with a jigsaw and add the finer detail with a fretsaw.

**5** Use a round-bladed knife to carefully separate the jacket and leg sections. Remove the double-sided sticky tape. The tape may break the surface a little, if so sand it clean with the rest of the parts.

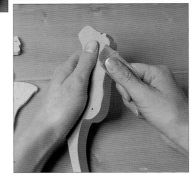

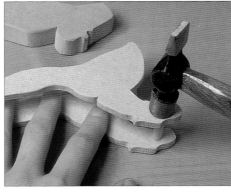

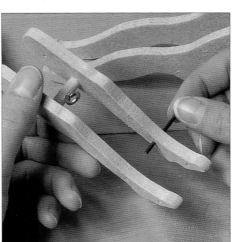

**7** Join the jacket pieces at the hands using the other cut length of dowel. Check it fits snugly over the body section, and that both sides are in line before gluing the dowel ends. When the glue is dry, sand the ends flush.

**8** Join the legs using the dowel with the screw eye. The screw eye must be horizontal and point towards the knees. Check that the hips are loose enough to move freely over the body and glue the dowel in place. Cut two lengths of wire slightly shorter than the leg span. Push them through the holes and glue in place. Fill the ends with wood filler and sand flush when dry.

**6** Cut two 3.5cm (1⅜in) lengths of 6mm (¼in) dowel. Drill a pilot hole in the centre of one and insert a small screw eye. Cut one 2cm (¾in) length and glue it into the hole at the base of the tail. Drill a pilot hole through the MDF at the base of the tail into the dowel and insert the other screw eye. The dowel will stop the screw working loose from the MDF.

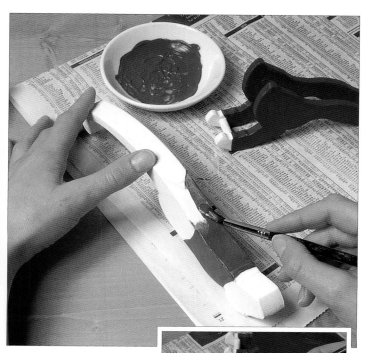

9 Prime all three parts with white paint. Allow to dry, then pencil in the outlines of the shoes and other details. Use strong flat colours to block in the main areas, then allow to dry before varnishing.

**10** Slide the jacket over the body and glue and pin in position. Use a pair of long nosed pliers to hold the wire pin steady, and tap into the hole. Seal in the wire with a spot of glue each end and hide with a blob of colour trailer.

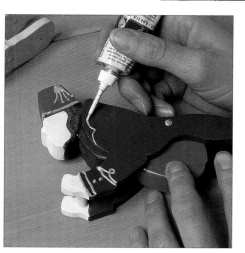

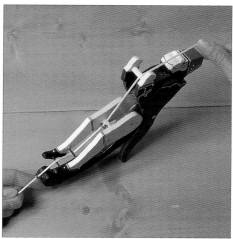

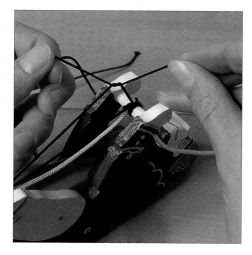

**11** Add fine detail and outlines with a colour trailer and a permanent marker. Cut a length of the wire slightly shorter than the width of the hips and attach the legs to the body by pushing this through the hip joints. Seal and cover as in step 10.

**12** Thread the nylon cord through the eyelet in the tail, over the wire bar in the feet, under the wire in the ankle, through the eyelet above the knees then around the front of the dowel between the monkey's hands.

**13** Bind the elastic tightly around the nylon cord joining it to the dowel between the hands. Take one end through the eyelet above the knees, pulling knees up to meet the arms, and tie off. Hang the monkey from a hook and pull and release the cord several times, if the monkey isn't climbing, the elastic is not tight enough around the nylon. Re-tie and try again. Once happy with the movement, seal knot with a spot of glue. Attach the pull ball to the bottom end of the nylon cord.

# FALLING MONKEY

## IN CARDBOARD

Balance one monkey arm on the top pin, drop the other to catch on the next pin down, then watch your monkey race to the bottom of the track.

### TOOLS & MATERIALS

- Cardboard boxes
- Newspaper, in two colours
- Coloured papers
- Tracing paper
- Large push pins
- Double-sided tape
- Masking tape
- PVA glue
- Paint
- Pencil and black pen
- Sharp craft knife
- Scissors
- Small decorating brush
- Artist's brush

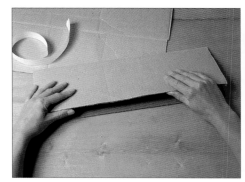

**1** Mark out four pieces of cardboard 44 x 15cm (17¼ x 6in), and two pieces 30 x 15cm (12 x 6in). Cut them out with a sharp craft knife. Stick the two smaller pieces together with double-sided sticky tape to make the base. Do the same with the others to make the front and back. The double layers will strengthen the toy.

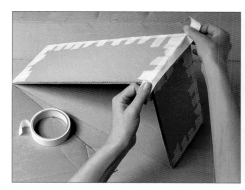

**2** Tape the pieces together into a wedge shape. Turn the wedge on its side and place on another cardboard piece. Draw around the wedge to mark out the side panel size. Cut out two single layer side triangles and tape to the wedge.

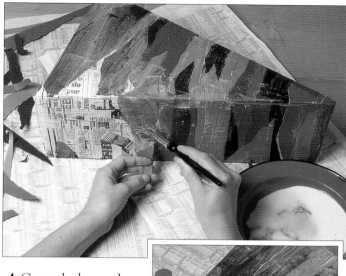

3 Trace the monkey outline on page 121 on to cardboard. Carefully cut out the monkey shape with sharp scissors.

4 Cover the box and monkey with two layers of newspaper strips, pasted on with PVA diluted 50 per cent with water. While wet, decorate the box with sky coloured paper strips. Finish with brighter leaf and fruit shapes. Dry, then sand off rough edges. Varnish with diluted PVA.

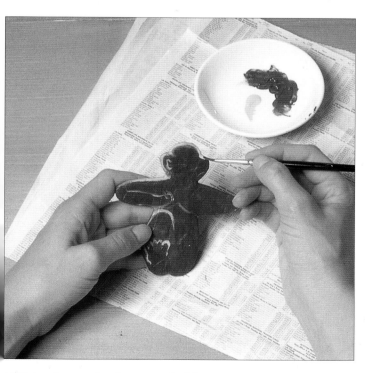

5 Paint the monkey brown and add details in a contrasting colour and a black pen.

6 Position the pins on the box. This is done by trial and error, as the positions will vary depending on how accurately the monkey is cut out. They will be roughly 8cm (3⅛in) apart vertically and 5.5cm (2⅛in) apart horizontally. Once you have found the best positions, glue the pins in place.

# COLOUR CHANGER

## IN PAPER

EASY

This toy is used by children the world over to tell fortunes or reveal a destiny written beneath the flaps. Ask a friend to choose a number, count out their choice on the changer, then they must choose from the colours or shapes then showing in the centre. Lift their chosen flap to reveal your secret message.

## TOOLS & MATERIALS
- Coloured paper squares
- Stickers, paints, pens or crayons to decorate

1 Fold the paper square corner to corner and crease the diagonals. Open out flat with the coloured side facing upwards.

2 Fold all four corners into the centre of the square and crease.

3 Turn the square over. Again fold all four corners to the centre.

4 Open the finished changer by sliding your thumbs and forefingers under the four flaps on the reverse side and pinching each corner to a point. Use coloured stckers or pens or to decorate or to write hidden messages under the flaps.

# FLYING BIRDS

## IN PAPER

These elegant birds are easily created with a few simple folds and careful creases in a square of paper. A simple hand movement makes it gently flap its wings. You could make lots of different coloured ones, add your own decoration, and string them up as a mobile hung in a window.

EASY

### TOOLS & MATERIALS

- 24cm (9½in) square of thin coloured paper
- 2 small bells and fine wire (optional)

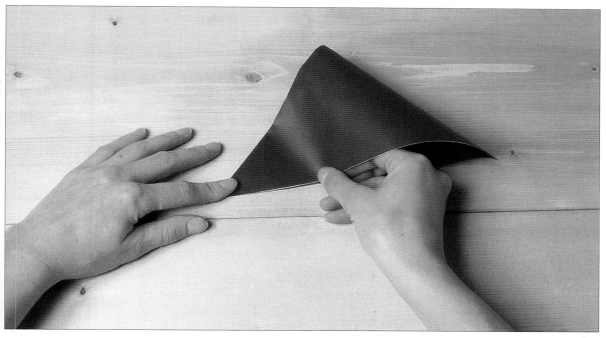

**1** Fold and crease the square of paper diagonally to make a triangle. Fold and crease this shape in half to make a smaller triangle.

**2** Open the second fold and hold the flap vertical. Slide your hand inside this flap and push out the sides, flattening the shape to form a square. Turn the paper over and again hold the triangular flap vertical, slide your hand inside and flatten into a neat square on top of the other square.

**3** With the closed neat corner at the top, fold the lower front edges into the centre and crease.

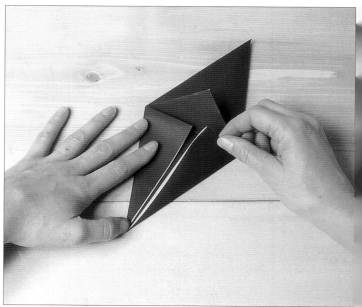

**4** Hold the point at the open end of the shape and lift the top layer upwards creasing the folds to form a diamond.

**5** Turn the paper over and repeat steps 3 and 4.

6 Starting a little below the centre, fold the lower points up and between the open edges of the diamond. This is known as a 'reverse fold'.

7 Fold one of these points downwards, between the crease, to form a head.

8 Hold the two lower points which form the underside of the body, between thumb and forefinger. Gently move your hands apart and together and see your finished bird take flight. For an additional touch, attach a small bell to each wing with fine wire.

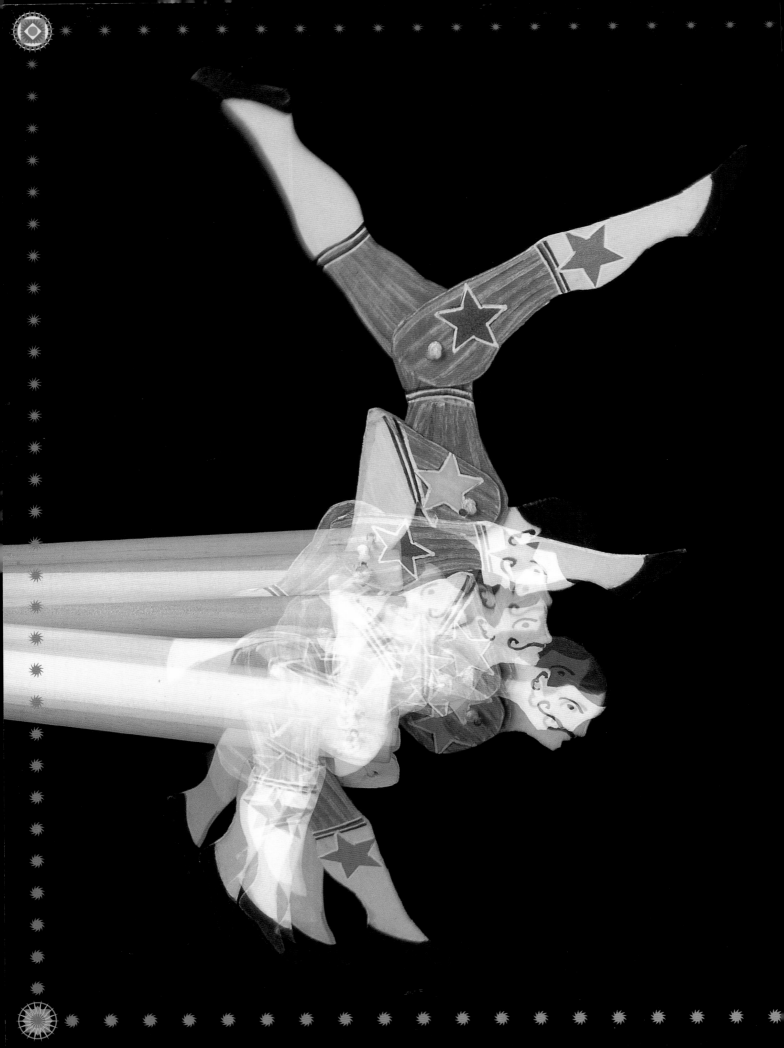

# Squeeze Acrobat

## IN CARD AND WOOD

INTERMEDIATE

This nineteenth-century style jointed acrobat is a star performer. Squeeze the bottom of the side poles together and make him somersault and tumble backwards and forwards. You can make it as simple or complicated as you like, this one is made of card but for a longer lasting toy, make it in wood.

## TOOLS & MATERIALS

- ◆ Tracing paper
- ◆ Plain white card 15 x 22cm (6 x 8¾in)
- ◆ Two 12mm (½in) dowel, 30cm (12in) long
- ◆ 6mm (¼in) dowel, 5.5cm (2⅛in) long
- ◆ Wooden bead
- ◆ Two short panel pins
- ◆ String
- ◆ Double-sided tape
- ◆ Coloured pencils

- ◆ Stick-on stars
- ◆ Scissors
- ◆ PVA glue
- ◆ Drill
- ◆ Drill bits: to match dowel sizes, and fine
- ◆ Hole punch
- ◆ Artist's brush
- ◆ Fine sandpaper
- ◆ Pin hammer
- ◆ Thin wire
- ◆ Wire tray
- ◆ Craft knife (optional)

1 Trace the outlines for the body, chest, arms and legs on page 122 on to plain white card. Make one body shape and two of each of the others, taking care to mark the hole positions. Cut out the shapes using scissors or a sharp knife. Carefully sandpaper any rough edges.

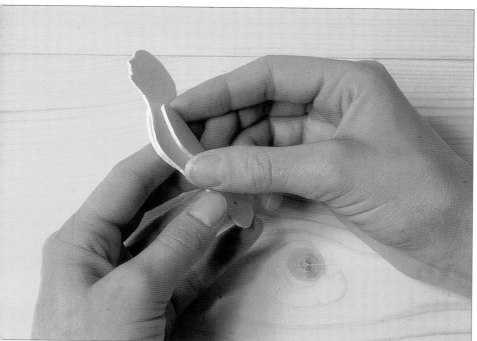

2 Stick the two chest pieces either side of the main body with double-sided sticky tape.

**3** Decorate both sides of the pieces using coloured pencils or crayons. Leave the lower arms and legs white to give the impression of an old fashioned bathing suit. Glue on stars to finish the decoration.

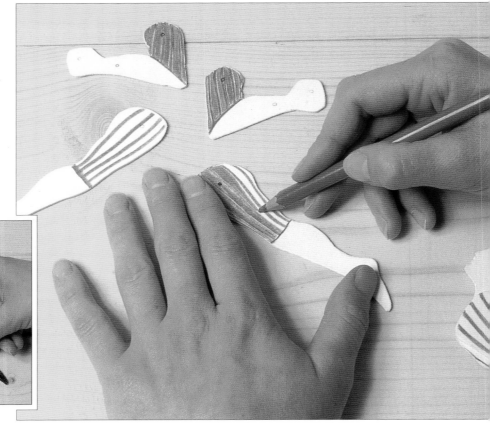

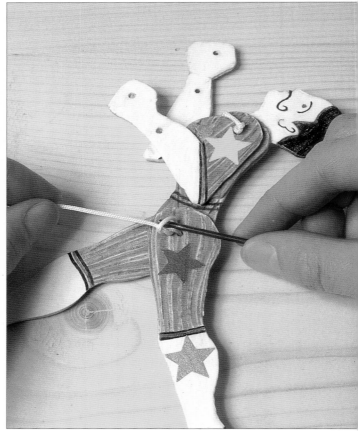

**4** Punch or drill out the holes slightly larger than the size of the string being used. Varnish the pieces with undiluted PVA and allow to dry on a wire tray.

**5** Tie a knot in one end of the string and join a leg to each side of the body with it. Tie the other end as close as possible to the body using a piece of wire and seal both knots with glue.

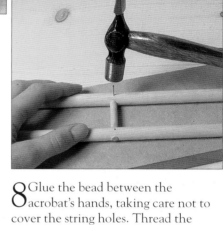

6 Drill a 6mm (¼in) hole 9cm (3½in) from the bottom of both side stick dowels. Use a home-made dowel vice to hold the dowels still (see page 10 – 11). This will be the fulcrum. Drill two small string holes side-by-side about 1cm (⅜in) from the other end of both sticks, parallel to the 6mm (¼in) holes.

7 Smear the end of the 6mm (¼in) dowel with glue and tap the dowel into the fulcrum holes. Drill fine pilot holes and pin the dowel firmly in place.

8 Glue the bead between the acrobat's hands, taking care not to cover the string holes. Thread the string through the front hole of one pole, on through the hands, then through the front hole on the second pole. Come back through the second hole, then through the arm holes, and on through the side stick. Leave a small amount of slack and tie a knot. Squeeze the bottom sticks gently together to test the movement. Adjust the amount of slack until the acrobat performs well, then seal the knot with a spot of glue.

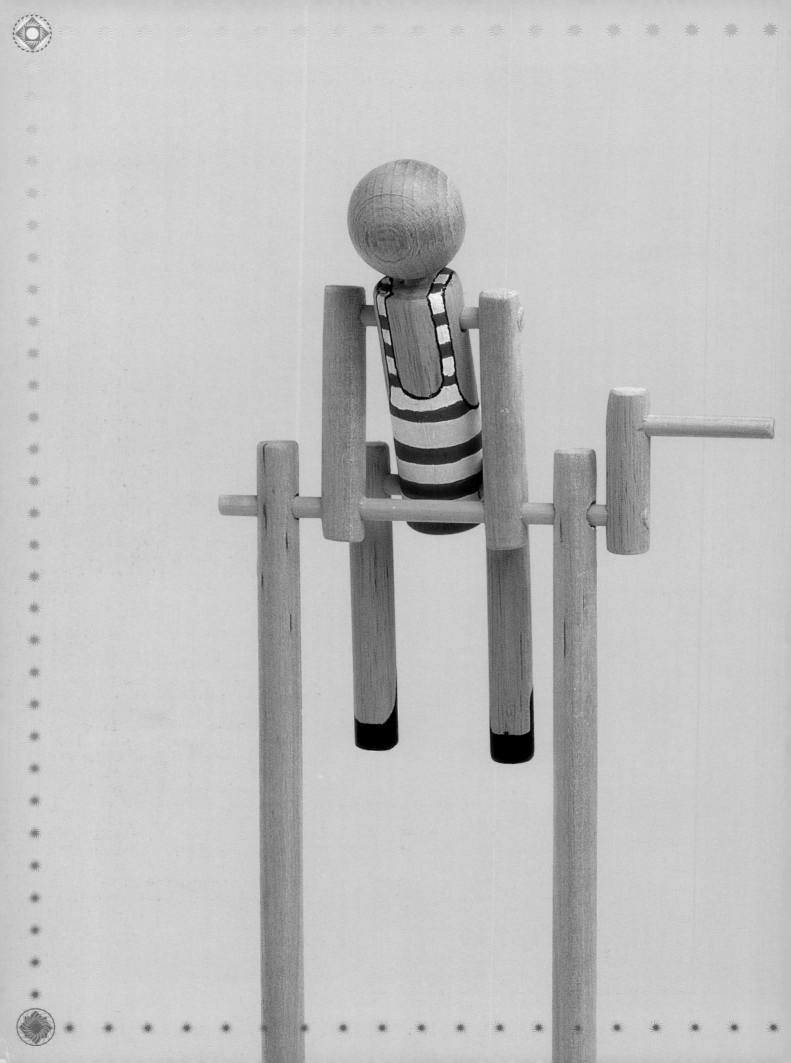

# WOODEN ACROBAT

## IN DOWEL AND BOARD

INTERMEDIATE

This acrobat might look more complicated to make than the one on the previous page, but it is in fact just as easy, although you do need more tools and materials. As with most toys, the more accurately you cut and drill, the better it will work.

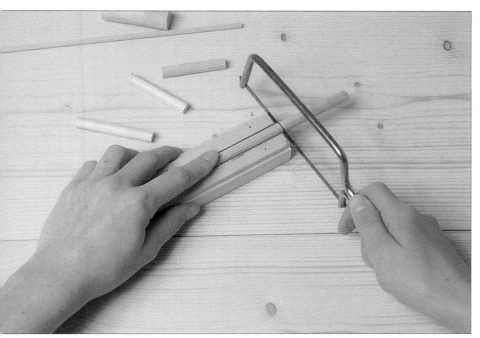

1 Cut the dowels into the appropriate lengths using the home-made dowel vice (see page 10) to hold the dowel steady while cutting.

2 Drill two 12mm (½in) holes 7cm (2¾in) apart through the base. Drill a 6mm (¼in) hole 16mm (⅝in) from the end of both the uprights and push them into the base plate with the holes to the top. Do not glue yet. Take the body section and drill one 6mm (¼in) hole for the shoulders and one parallel for the hip joint. Secure the head with dowel, by drilling a 6mm (¼in) hole in the ball and in the body. Take care not to drill into the shoulder joint. Glue the dowel neck in position. Drill a 6mm (¼in) hole through each leg 12mm (½in) from the top. The arms have a 6mm (¼in) hole drilled through the shoulders and hands as close as possible to the ends. The winder arm has a 6mm (¼in) hole drilled at each end.

**3** Paint on a leotard and shoes with acrylic paints as shown. Alternatively, leave the figure plain and simply finish the wood with wax polish.

**4** Glue one side of the hip dowel into one leg and push the hip joint through the body section, then glue the other leg in position. Make sure it allows a free movement of the legs.

**5** Treat the shoulder joint the same way as the hip joint, check that both arms and legs run parallel to one another. Set the acrobat aside until the glue is dry. Glue the winder and hand bar assembly together and leave to dry.

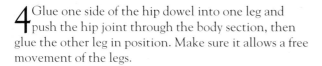

**6** Slide the winder first through one upright, then through both the acrobat's hands. Push through the other upright then adjust so that the winder turns freely. Glue the uprights to the base, and the hands to the hand bar. Leave until the glue has set.

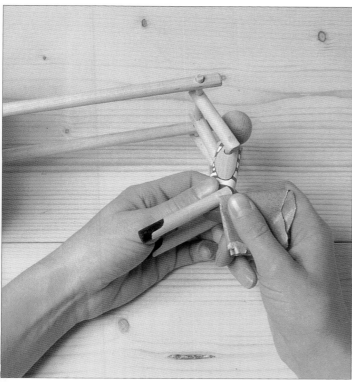

**7** Clean any rough edges with sandpaper. Finish with a coat of wax polish.

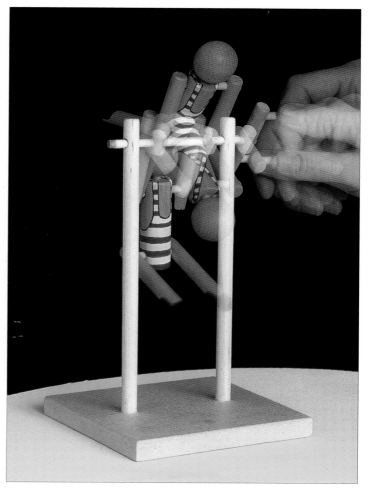

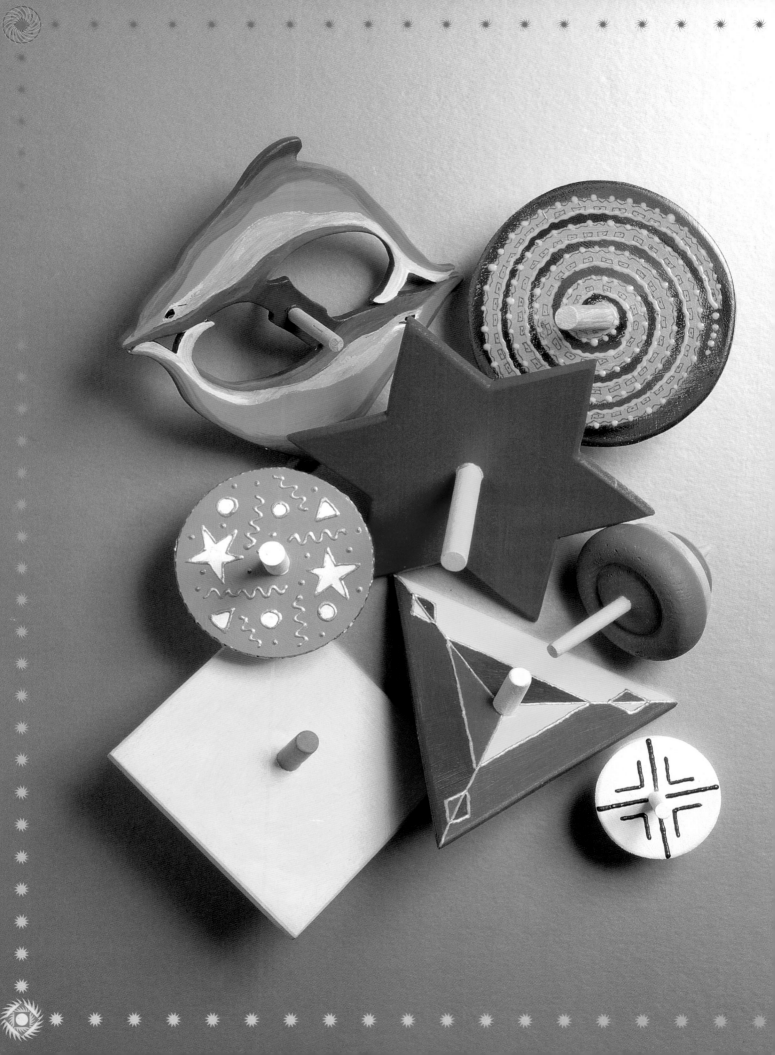

# Spinning Tops

## IN CARD AND WOOD

EASY

Spinning tops have been a favourite children's toy in almost every culture on Earth. Tops have been found that date back to 2000BC. This simple one can be made in minutes and can be spun with the fingers or by using the pull-string launcher.

### TOOLS & MATERIALS

- Thick card, 10cm (4in) square
- Hexagonal pencil
- 8mm (⁵⁄₁₆in) dowel 15cm (6in) long for launcher
- Two 16mm (⁵⁄₈in) screw eyelets
- 6mm (¼in) dowel 5cm (2in) long
- Cord or string, 50cm (19⁵⁄₈in) long

- Coloured pencil crayons
- Fine sandpaper
- Compass
- Scissors
- Drill
- Drill bits: to match the dowel sizes, and fine
- Craft knife
- Bradawl

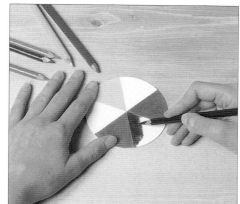

*Tops come in all shapes, sizes and colours, so don't feel restricted to any of them. The small selection shown left have all been made from offcuts and left-over bits from other projects in the book. Try making a six sided top, add numbers, and use it in board games instead of a dice.*

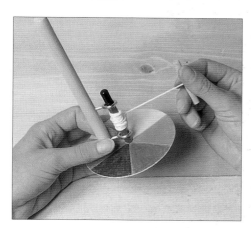

**1** Draw a circle onto the card using a compass. Leaving the compass at the same setting, place the tip and the pencil point on the edge of the circle and make a mark. Move the compass point to that mark and repeat until the circle is divided into six equal parts. Draw lines joining all the points to the centre.

**2** Use coloured pencils in primary and secondary colours to decorate the circle as a colour wheel.

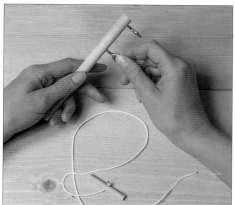

**3** Cut a hexagonal pencil to 10cm (4in) in length using a sharp craft knife. Drill a hole about one third of the way down the pencil. Use a drill large enough to allow the cord or string to pass through freely. Sharpen the pencil and push this end through the centre of the wheel.

**4** Make two pilot holes 5cm (2in) apart in one end of the thicker dowel, using a drill or bradawl. Screw in the eyelets, leaving the holes running parallel to the stick. Drill a small hole through the 5cm (2in) length of dowel. Pass the string through the hole and secure with a knot to make a handle.

**5** Push the pencil through the eyelets and the other end of string through the pencil. Wind the string around the pencil and pull sharply while holding the stick, to release the spinning top.

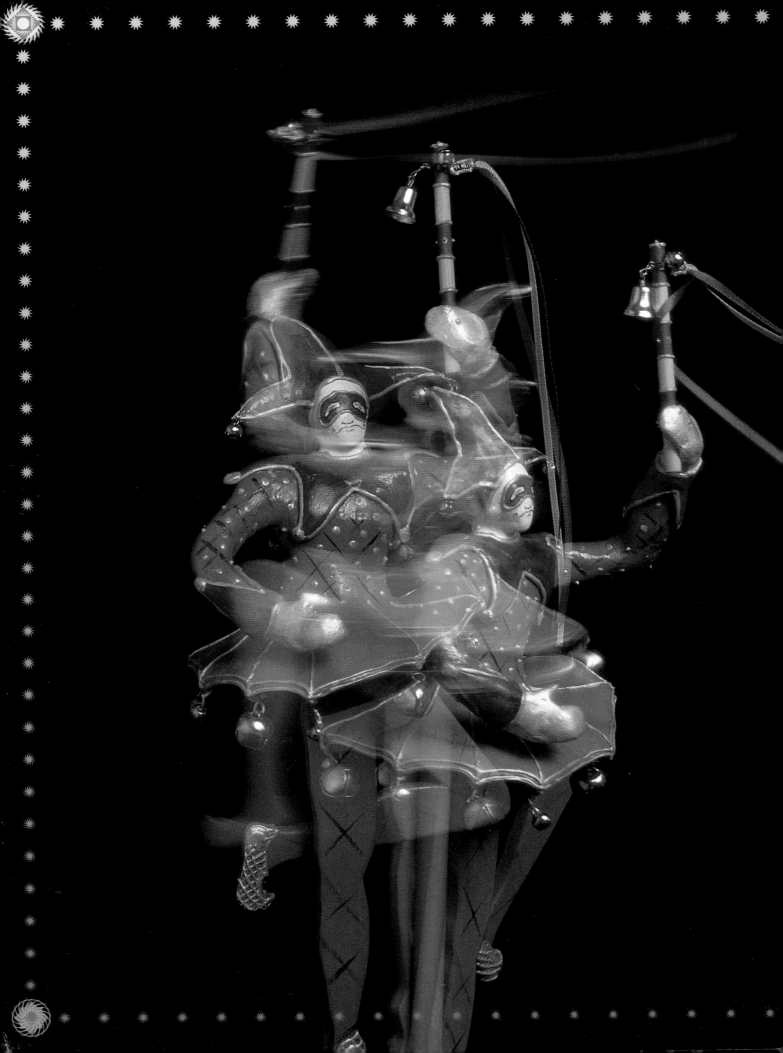

# SPINNING HARLEQUIN

## IN AIR DRYING CLAY

Introduce yourself to the art of sculpture by following the instructions below. It takes a little time and patience to make this beautifully detailed dancing character but you'll be surprised at the ease with which your figures manipulate the clay and a figure starts to emerge.

## TOOLS & MATERIALS

- ◆ Thin card and tracing paper
- ◆ Sculptor's mesh, 30 x 20cm (12 x 8in)
- ◆ One packet air drying clay (DAS)
- ◆ 10mm (⅜in) dowel, 40cm (15¾in)
- ◆ 6mm (¼in) dowel, 10cm (4in) long
- ◆ 6mm (¼in) dowel, 8cm (3⅛in) long
- ◆ 6mm (¼in) MDF or plywood, 20 x 10cm (8 x 4in)
- ◆ 12mm (½in) softwood, 7cm (2¾in) square
- ◆ Two small wooden balls
- ◆ Wooden door knob
- ◆ 6cm (2⅜in) diameter wooden wheel
- ◆ Medium gauge copper wire
- ◆ Nylon cord 30cm(12in)

- ◆ Small washer
- ◆ Wood glue
- ◆ 15 amp fuse wire
- ◆ Ribbon
- ◆ Two sizes of brass bells
- ◆ White emulsion paint
- ◆ Acrylic or poster paint
- ◆ Wax polish
- ◆ Polyurethane varnish
- ◆ Gold relief liner
- ◆ Artist's brushes
- ◆ Fine sandpaper
- ◆ Scissors
- ◆ Glue gun
- ◆ Protective mask and goggles
- ◆ Drill
- ◆ Drill bits: to match dowel sizes, 3mm (⅛in), 12mm (½in), the largest bit available and fine
- ◆ Fretsaw
- ◆ Clamp
- ◆ Pliers
- ◆ Craft knife

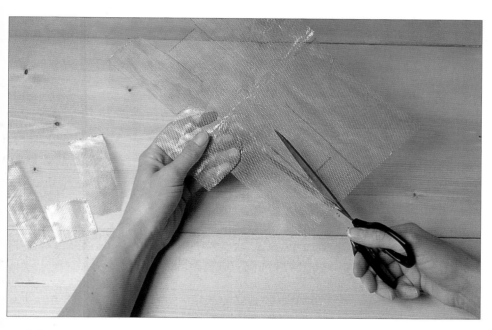

**1** Make templates of the figure and legs from the trace-offs on page 123. Place the figure template onto the sculptor's mesh and draw around it. Cut out the figure with sharp scissors.

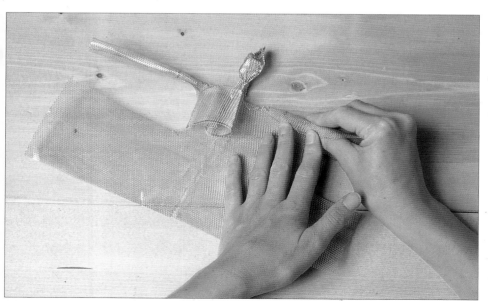

**2** Begin to mould the frame of the figure starting with the head. Bring the edges of the top section in towards the centre, moulding the mesh with your fingers, to form an oval. Make the arms by rolling the edges of the second flaps inwards, so the horizontals meet to form a cylinder for each arm.

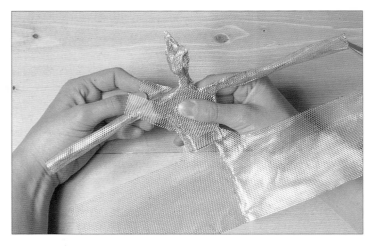

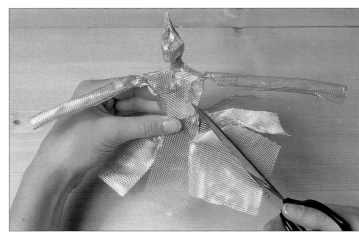

3 Now roll the next sections in towards the centre, coiling the mesh to make a body. Use small strips of mesh to repair any mistakes by simply moulding a piece over the damaged area.

4 Make the skirt from the final panel of mesh. Roll into a cylinder, and use scissors to cut lines up to the waist. Pull the cut sections outwards forming an umbrella. Trim off the edges of the mesh to the size and shape required.

5 Flatten the ends of the arms to make hands. Bend the left arm up towards the head, and the other to curve down.

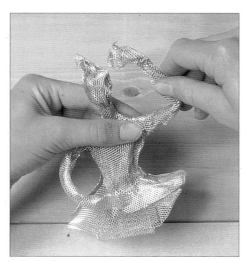

6 Working from the head down, use your fingers to push small pieces of clay into the mesh, gradually building up the form. Use water to keep the clay workable and the surface smooth.

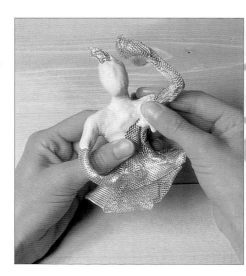

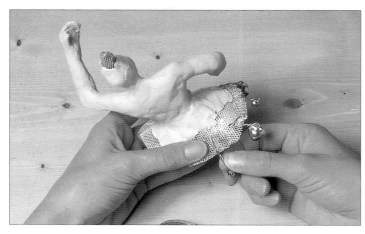

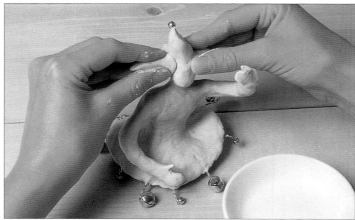

7 Thread the bells onto lengths of fuse wire. Push the wires through the edge of the skirt mesh, twisting the ends together to hold the bells in place. Cover the top and the under side of the skirt with clay, leaving a hole in the centre large enough to take the dowel rod.

8 Roll a small ball of clay between your palms. Flatten one end and bring the other to a point, to form a cone. Make four of these and use a little water to mould them to the head to create a hat for the harlequin. Use fuse wire to attach a bell to the top point. The other three bells will be attached at a later stage to avoid weakening the structure.

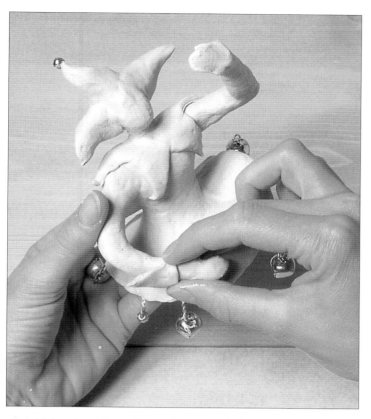

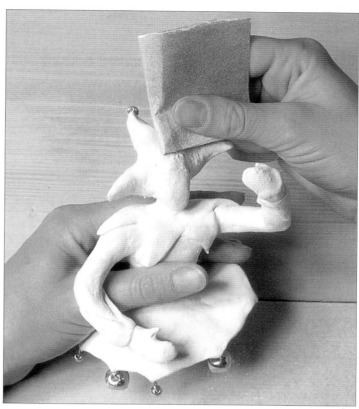

9 Add details with a collar and cuffs made from triangles of rolled out clay. Bond these to the jacket with a little water. Leave the model figure to dry thoroughly.

10 Remove any rough spots and reshape any errors with fine sandpaper. Use a fine drill bit to make holes to attach the wired bells to the three remaining points on the hat.

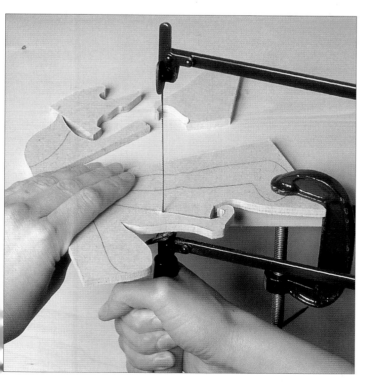

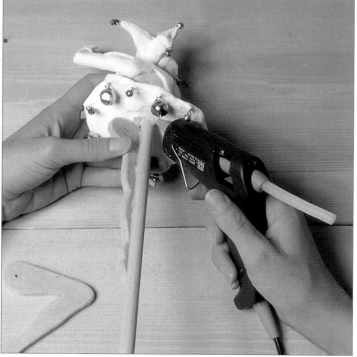

11 Use the templates to draw the legs onto the MDF. Put on the mask, clamp the wood to a solid surface and cut out with a fretsaw. Drill the hip joints using a drill bit slightly thicker than the copper wire. Sand the legs to a smooth finish.

12 Push the dowel centre pole up inside the figure. Glue the straight leg in position onto the pole using a hot glue gun. Secure the pole to the body by filling the hole with glue. Leave the glue to dry, then cover over the glued area with small pieces of clay.

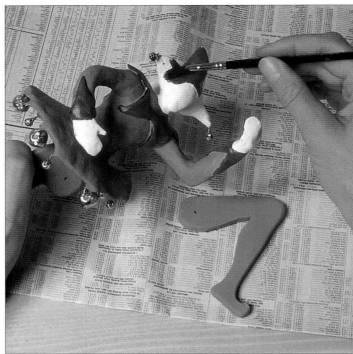

**13** Prime all the pieces with a coat of white emulsion and allow to dry. Begin to decorate the figure by painting the body and the stick with a flat base colour.

**14** Paint the hat, collar and cuffs in a contrasting colour. Use a fine brush to create a fishnet pattern on the body and legs.

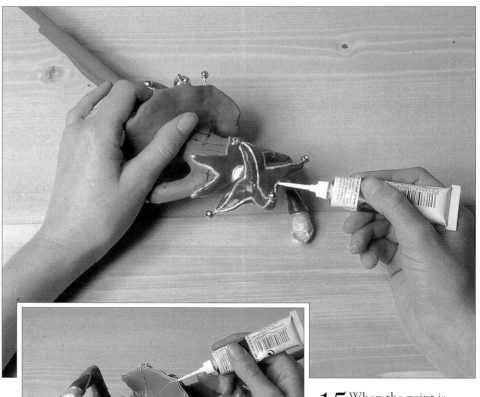

**15** When the paint is thoroughly dry, carefully add the fine detail to the costume and shoes with gold relief liner.

**16** Join the legs at the hip with the length of copper wire. Coil it over at one end, and push the other through the right hip, through a small washer that acts as a spacer, then through the other hip. Hold in place by bending the wire with a pair of pliers.

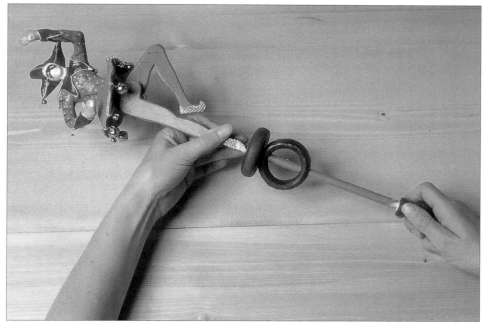

**17** Use the largest drill bit available to make a hole in the centre of the 7cm (2¾in) softwood square. Whittle the piece into a ring with a sharp craft knife, then drill a 12mm (½in) hole vertically through the ring.

**18** Paint the ring, wheel, door knob and balls. Drill a 10mm (⅜in) hole in the centre of the wheel and thread onto the 10mm (⅜in) dowel until the harlequin's foot rests on it. Glue in position. Slide the ring onto the rod until it touches the wheel. Make a 3mm (⅛in) hole horizontally through one side of the ring and through the dowel. Drill a 10mm (⅜in) hole into the flat end of the door knob and glue onto the end of the dowel. Varnish the whole toy. Once dry, apply a coat of wax polish to the underside of the wheel, the dowel inside the ring and the top of the ring to make running smoother.

**19** Drill a 6mm (¼in) hole halfway into each of the wooden balls and paint them with your chosen colour. When dry, glue one on each end of an 8cm (3⅛in) length of 6mm (¼in) dowel, and drill a small hole through the centre of the bar. Tie and seal a knot in one end of 30cm (12in) of cord. Thread the cord through the hole in the pull bar, through the hole in the side of the ring and through the centre pole hole. Tie and seal the knot. Finish by gluing a wand, cut from a 10cm (4in) length of 6mm (¼in) dowel and decorated with a bell, paint and ribbons. Put into his hand. Wind up the string and pull to see your harlequin spin.

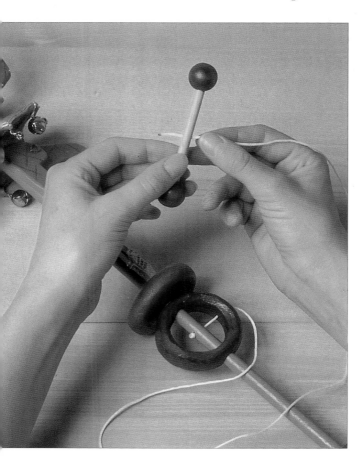

# WINDMILLS

## IN PAPER

EASY

These bright and colourful windmills are easy to make and beautiful to watch in motion. Made in different sizes and colours and turning together as a group, this simple design becomes a mesmerising sight.

### TOOLS & MATERIALS

- Two sheets coloured paper 24 cm (9½in) square
- Any size dowel, 30cm (12in) long
- Double-sided tape
- Compass
- Ruler
- Scissors
- Pencil
- Eyelet
- Large push pin
- Pin hammer

**1** Stick two colours of paper back to back and cut to a square of 24cm (9½in). Find the centre of the square by drawing a pencil line corner to corner diagonally across the paper. Place the compass point where the lines cross and draw a circle 14cms (5½in) in diameter.

**2** Measure 7cms (2¾in) to the left of each corner and mark the point. Place the compass point on the edge of the circle and the pencil tip to the marked point. Draw an arc, joining the two points together. Cut along these lines.

**3** Rub out the guide lines and make a small hole 1cm (⅜in) diagonally from each corner. Fold all four corners to the centre, securing each one on top of the last with a small piece of double-sided tape. Do not crease the folds.

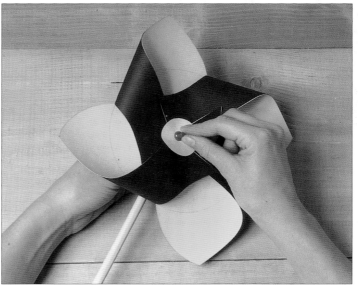

**4** Fit the eyelet to the centre of the windmill, pushing it through all the corner holes. Gently tap the eyelet in place with a hammer.

**5** Cut a circle of coloured paper for the centre. Use a large, coloured pin pushed through the paper and the eyelet to secure the windmill to the dowel, leaving enough slack to allow it to spin in the breeze.

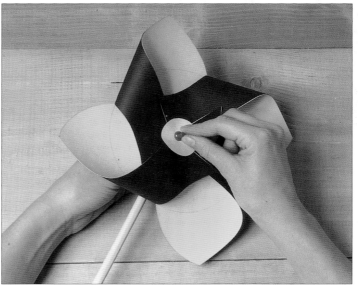

# THE WOODCUTTER

## IN WOOD AND PLYWOOD

HARD

There was a time when no cottage garden was complete without a weather-vane or wind-gauge. This whittled woodchopper will go on chopping logs for years, through summer sun and winter rain, demanding only the occasional coat of varnish.

**1** Make templates of the arms, shoulder spacer, body and sail from the trace-offs on page 124. Use the templates to draw the arms and shoulder spacer onto the 6mm (¼in) plywood. Use the body template to mark out the figure onto the piece of softwood, avoiding knots which are difficult to cut and whittle around.

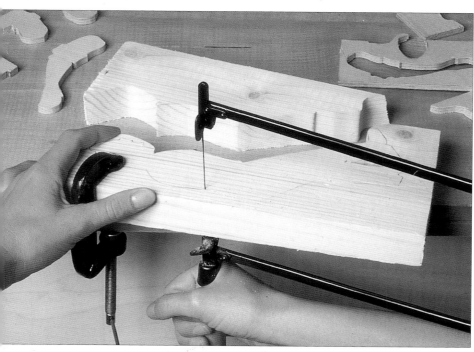

**2** Clamp the wood to the bench and use a fretsaw to cut around all the shapes. Do not worry if the body cutting is not accurate, it can be whittled into shape.

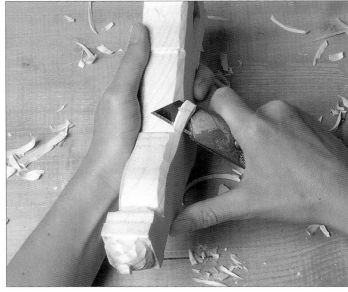

**3** Measure 5cm (2in) down from each corner of the base and saw off the corners. Draw a line 19mm (¾in) from one end, and mark the upright positions with crosses 5cm (2in) apart. Drill with a 16mm (⅝in) bit. To ensure the holes are drilled at right-angles to the base, use a drill stand or a home-made jig. Paint the base on both sides with flat colour and leave to dry.

**4** Take the body piece and gently whittle – don't hack – away the hard edges. Avoid digging into the grain and make sure the blade is sharp. Replace the blade if it begins to blunt. Whittle away at the nose, chin and hat until you are happy with the result. Leave the cut marks showing, after all this is a piece of rustic carving.

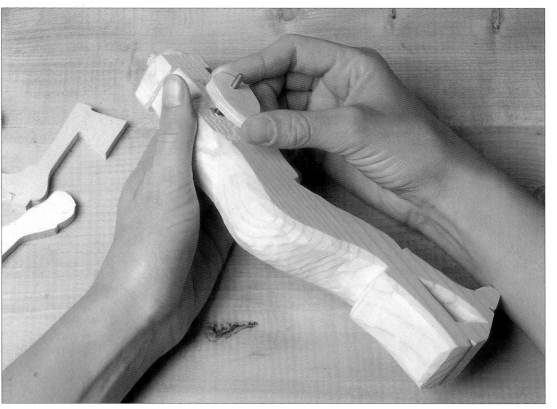

**5** Drill a hole through the shoulders of the body section with a 3mm (⅛in) drill bit. Enlarge the hole o[n] the left side to take the bol[t] head, and countersink it on the other shoulder to take the nut. Insert the bolt and tighten until the nut is flus[h] with the body, then lock th[e] nut with glue. Drill a 3mm (⅛in) hole in the shoulder spacer, feed it over the bolt[,] then glue and pin it in position over the nut. Drill two 3mm (⅛in) holes in the axe arm, one at the shoulde[r] and one just above the elbow for the drive.

6 Start to decorate the piece. To make the most of the wood grain, use very diluted water-based colours to allow the grain to show through. Add shadows by darkening areas that would be creased, and make highlights by lifting off colour with a damp cloth.

7 Leave the arms, hands and face natural wood, this will give good flesh tone when varnished. Paint the boots a strong black and give the shirt a base coat of white. Allow the paint to dry then add detail to the shirt and axe with a fine brush. Give the arms and the body at least two coats of polyurethane varnish. Pay particular attention to the areas that cannot be reached when the toy is finished, like the shoulder joints and the bottom of the feet.

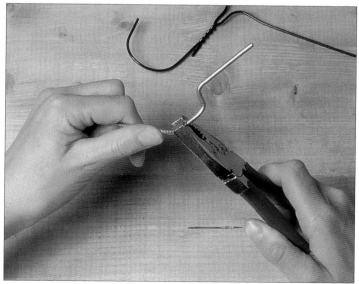

8 Cut one of the bolts down to 10mm (⅜in) in length and attach it to the axe arm elbow with a nut. Put two washers on to the shoulder bolt, then the arm, followed by another washer, and finally a nut. Tighten the nut leaving enough slack for the arm to swing freely, then seal the nuts with a spot of glue.

9 Form a loop in both ends of a 24cm (9½in) length of coathanger wire using long nosed pliers. Make a right angled bend about 4cm (1⅝in) from one end of the welding rod, and continue until a 'U' shape is formed and the main shafts are back in line.

**10** Drill a 3mm (⅛in) hole 3cm (1⅛in) from the end of each of the two dowel uprights. Thread the straight length of coathanger wire (the power take-off) onto the bent welding rod (drive shaft). Push a dowel upright onto either end of the drive shaft. Tap the uprights into the base, making sure the drive shaft moves freely.

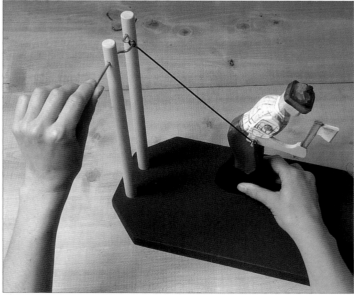

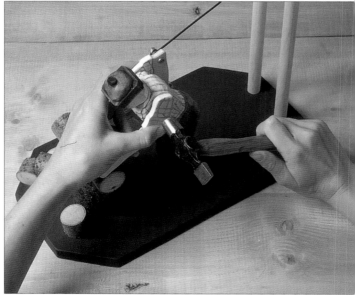

**11** Attach the power take-off loosely to the figure and establish, by trial and error, the position which gives it the best movement. Draw around the feet, remove the figure and drill a pilot hole through the base. Reposition the figure and drill through the pilot hole in the base, into the feet. Glue and screw figure in position.

**12** Connect the power take-off to the axe arm by placing a washer each side of the loop and tighten the nut. Leaving enough slack for free movement of the arm, seal the nut with glue. Cut the logs to appropriate lengths, then glue and pin them to the base. Position the left arm steadying a log, and glue and pin at the shoulder.

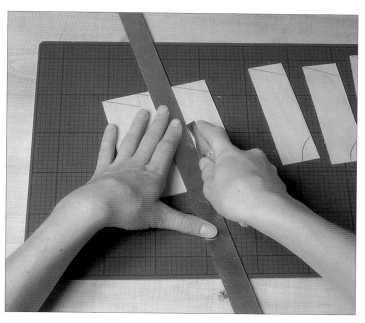

**13** To make the sails, use a sharp, strong blade and a steel rule to cut the 1.5mm (1⁄16in) ply into eight 4cm (1⅝in) strips marked out from the template.

**14** Divide the wheel into eight equal sections with a pencil and ruler. Repeat on the reverse side, making the segments roughly 10mm (⅜in) out of line with each other, and join the lines diagonally across the edge. Clamp the wheel into a vice and saw across the edge to a depth of 10mm (⅜in). Repeat with the other seven marks. Glue the sails in position and leave to dry.

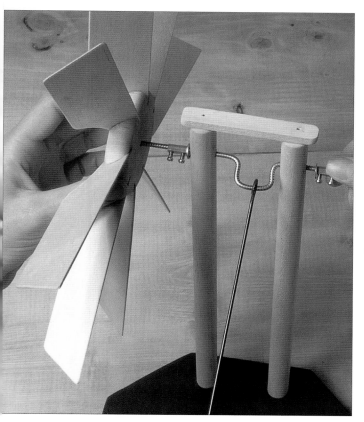

**15** Pin and glue the plywood strip to the top of the uprights. Put a washer on each end of the drive shaft and hold it loosely in position with a brass collar cut from the electric jointing block. Slip the propeller onto the shaft and glue in position. Adjust the uprights until the prop runs true, before gluing them to the base. Trim off the ends of the drive shaft, and paint the whole toy with two coats of polyurethane outdoor varnish.

# AIRPLANES

## IN PAPER

EASY

## TOOLS & MATERIALS
◆ A4 sheets of paper    ◆ Scissors

These are just three simple examples from a vast airforce of paper planes. As a general rule, the neater you fold them, the better they fly, so make sure you make them carefully. Use coloured paper to give them added interest, or colour the paper before folding.

## THE CLASSIC DART

Probably the original paper airplane. The simplicity, beauty and performance of this dart have no equal.

1 Fold the paper in half lengthways, crease and open out. Lift the two front corners and fold them to meet the centre

2 Fold the edges made by step 1 to meet the centre crease. Try to keep the nose point sharp.

3 Fold the outside edges together and reflatten the first crease.

4 Fold the outside edge down to meet the centre crease, turn the plane over and repeat the fold on this side.

5 Open the wings up to about ninety degrees, and cut a small section off the nose to make it safe to throw. To achieve maximum distance, launch the dart firmly at a slightly upwards angle, adjust the angle of the wings until you achieve the best results. Thrown properly it will travel 10 to 15m (11 to 16½yds).

# THE SWEPTBACK WING

The performance of this plane can be altered by opening the wing pockets slightly to increase the angle of attack, which will increase lift.

**1** Fold the short edge to meet the long edge and crease. Carefully cut off the remaining section and fold it in half lengthways, this will become the tail.

**2** Fold the triangle in half to make a small triangle, and unfold. Then fold the two loose corners down to meet the centre line.

**3** Slide the tail strip underneath the triangular flaps. Fold the front corners across to meet the lower point of the triangular flaps.

**4** Fold the plane in half, top sides together. Fold one wing back one side, and the other on the other side, dividing the tail section in half. Open the wings to ninety degrees.

**5** Snip a small section off the nose for safety. Launch the plane with a firm thrust and watch it fly.

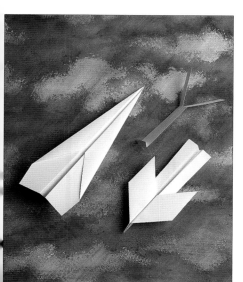

# THE HELICOPTER

This is the simplest of all flying shapes and takes seconds to make.

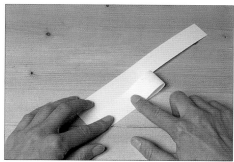

**1** Take a strip of paper and cut it down the middle to just short of half way. Bend the two flaps outwards.

**2** Make two small folds in the outer end to give it downwards stability. The amount of spin and rate of descent depends on the angle of the flaps. Launch by dropping it from as high as possible.

# PARACHUTIST

## IN FABRIC AND COLOURED MODELLING CLAY

EASY

This toy takes minutes to make and gives hours of fun. Thrown high into the air or dropped from above, the canopy fills out as the parachute sails down to land its passenger gently on the ground. Children will love playing with it and so will you.

### TOOLS & MATERIALS

- ◆ 40cm (15¾in) square dressmaker's nylon lining fabric
- ◆ 3m (3yd 9½in) thin nylon cord or string

- ◆ Modelling clay
- ◆ PVA glue
- ◆ Masking tape
- ◆ Pencil
- ◆ Drawing pin
- ◆ Scissors
- ◆ Bradawl

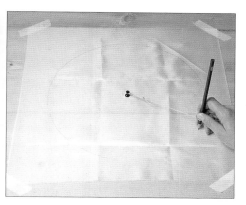

**1** Lie the fabric on a flat surface and secure in place with masking tape. Cut a 20cm (8in) length of cord, tie one end round the pencil and pin the other to the centre of the fabric, leaving about 17.5cm (6⅞in) of cord between the pencil and the pin. Stretch the cord taut, keep the pencil upright and draw a circle on the fabric, using the tension of the cord as a guide.

**2** Divide the circle into six equal parts. To do this, place the pin and pencil point with the string taut on the circumference of the circle. Mark the point the pencil touches, then move the pin to that point. Continue to mark around the circle until back at the beginning. Move 10mm (⅜in) in towards the centre and dot each point with a small amount of PVA glue and allow to dry.

**3** Cut out the circle with a pair of scissors, then pierce the fabric through the dry PVA with a bradawl. Cut a small circle in the centre of the fabric. This will help the parachute fall by allowing the air to stream through its canopy.

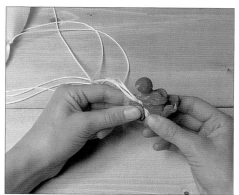

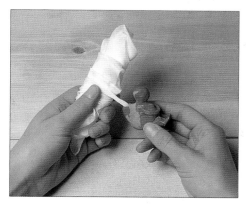

**4** Cut the cord into six 40cm (15¾in) lengths and thread them through the holes, securing with a knot. Gather the loose ends together and tie them together with a knot.

**5** Take a small ball of modelling clay and roll it between your palms. Mould it into your chosen figure and pinch it onto the gathered strings.

**6** Roll up the canopy and wrap the strings around it. Throw your parachute high into the air and watch it fall gently down to the ground.

# THE WOODPECKER

## IN PLASTIC MODELLING CLAY

INTERMEDIATE

The frantic pecking of this woodpecker as he descends his pole is quite hypnotic. It is surprisingly simple to make with a few craft materials and tools. Make your woodpecker as colourful as you wish so that he is king of the forest.

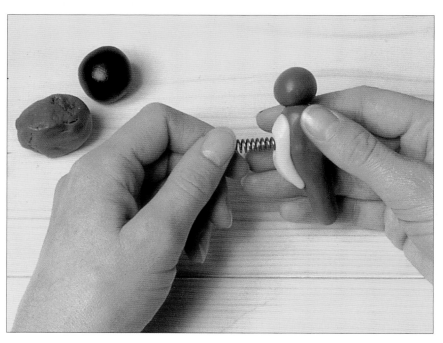

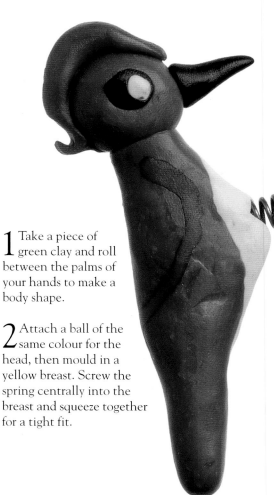

**1** Take a piece of green clay and roll between the palms of your hands to make a body shape.

**2** Attach a ball of the same colour for the head, then mould in a yellow breast. Screw the spring centrally into the breast and squeeze together for a tight fit.

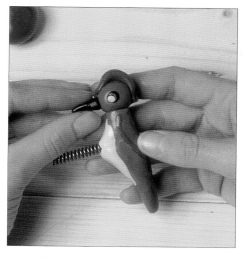

3 Add detail and features by pushing different colours into the background colour. Bake in a hot oven following the manufacturer's instructions.

4 Put on the protective goggles and mask. Use the rod-size drill bit to make a hole right through the centre of the base. Drill through one of the small balls, and half way through the other. Use a home-made ball vice to keep the balls steady (see page 11). With the same drill, make a hole through the larger ball. Ease the drill through a few times until the welding rod just passes through. Drill a spring-sized hole at right angles to the rod, almost half way through the ball, taking care not to reach the rod.

5 When the bird has cooled down, screw the spring into the hole. Glue the half-drilled ball to the top of the pole. Slide the other on below the bird to act as a stop, then glue the pole into the base. Flick the tail and watch the bird descend the pole. If the bird is too large, a double vibration can set up, and the bird will stop. Just steady the pole and away it will go again.

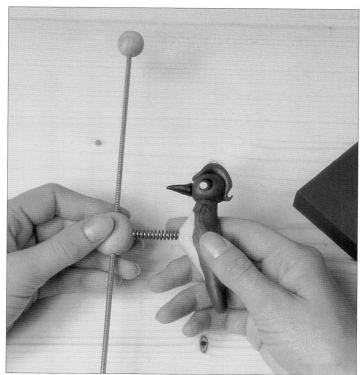

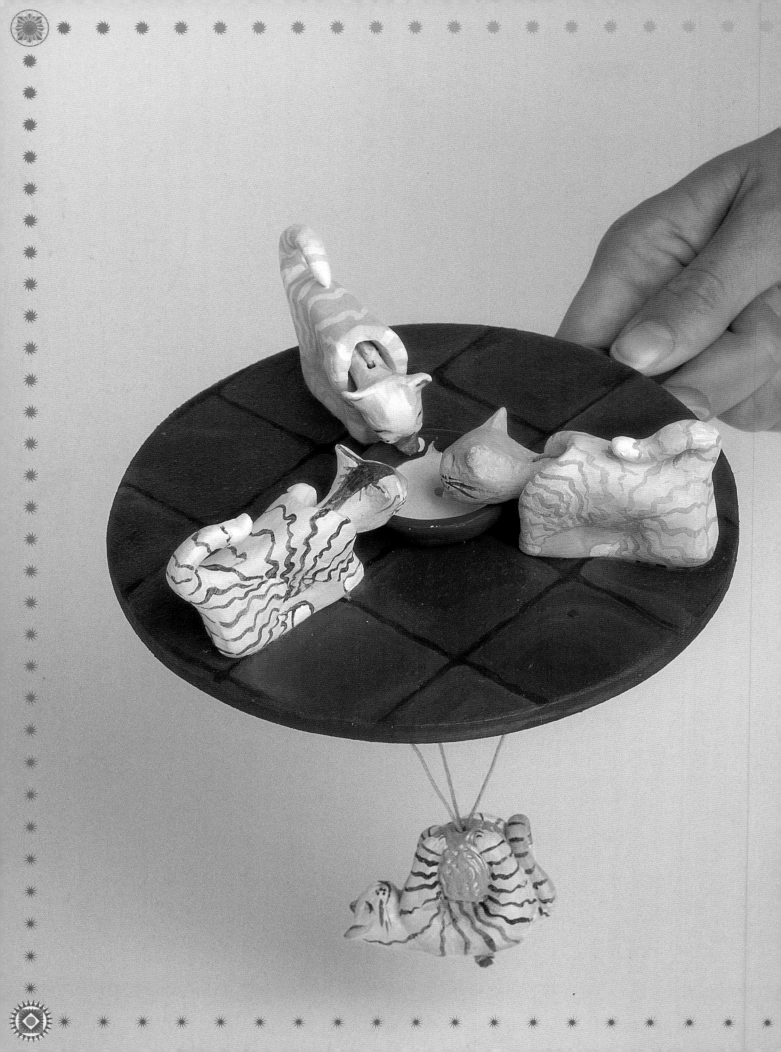

# DRINKING CATS

## IN EPOXY PUTTY

HARD

"Can we get a cat pleeease!" If this is a familiar echo around your home then look no further. Make these feline friends and sit back and relax while they feed themselves.

## TOOLS & MATERIALS

- Two packets epoxy putty (Milliputt)
- 6mm (¼in) MDF or plywood, 18cm (7⅛in) square
- 12 x 6mm (½ x ¼in) flat dowel, 14cm (5½in)
- Copper wire, 6cm (2⅜in)
- Glue
- Two panel pins
- Strong string
- White emulsion paint
- Water-based paints
- Water-based varnish
- Protective gloves
- Protective mask and goggles
- Jigsaw
- Drill
- Drill bits: 6mm (¼in), one slightly thicker than the copper wire
- Modelling tool
- Artist's brush

**1** Make up the epoxy putty, following the instructions on the packet. Wear gloves to protect your hands. Use one pack at a time as once mixed the epoxy putty will start to harden. Roll the putty into a sausage and divide equally to make two cats. Repeat for the other two cats.

**2** Take one ball of the putty and divide into two, taking one third for the head and the rest for the body. Roll the larger piece into a sausage, and bend to an arch. Pinch the centre between thumb and forefinger to form the body of the cat, the pinched section separating the back and front legs.

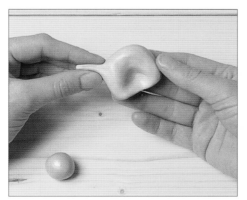

**3** Draw out a tail from one end of the shape, and flatten the other end with your thumb.

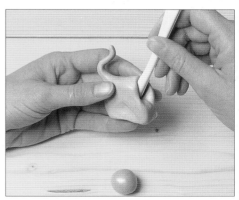

**4** Use a modelling tool or the wrong end of a small paintbrush to form a hole for the cat's neck to fit into. Elongate the top and bottom of the hole to allow for the nodding movement.

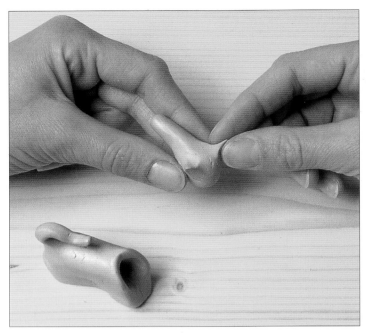

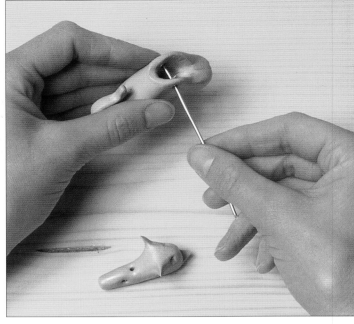

5 Roll the remaining third of the putty into a ball, and pinch one side out to form a neck, checking for size against the body. Pinch out two ears and a tongue to form the face. Smooth out any imperfections with a small amount of water on your fingertips. Model a dish large enough for three cats to drink from, by pushing a thumb into a small ball of putty and dragging up the sides. Make the pendulum which hangs beneath the base either as a cat or a ball, adding fine detail with a modelling tool.

6 Before the putty hardens, use wire to make five holes. To make the first two holes in the head section for the string, push the wire through the back of the neck, just behind the ears, and exit through the throat. The second hole, just behind the first, runs at right angles to it – this is the pivot point. Move to the body and make a hole through the shoulders for the fulcrum wire, make sure the neck section has room to move freely. Make a hole running up through the base and into the neck cavity – this is for the string. The last hole is through the pendulum, large enough to take three thicknesses of the string. Leave the models about three hours to harden.

7 Sand the base of each cat so it can stand flat, then give each model a coat of white emulsion paint.

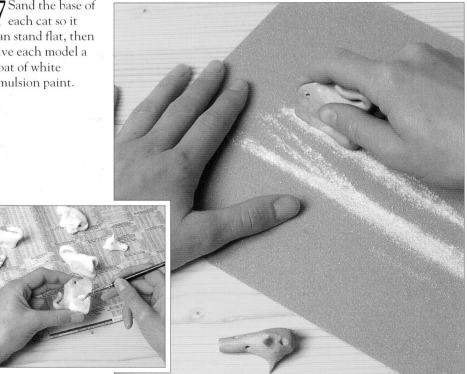

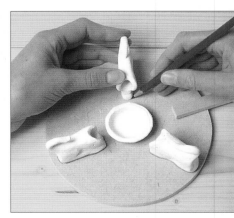

8 Put on the protective mask and goggles Use a jigsaw to cut a disc approximately 16cms (6¼in) in diameter from the MDF. Position the cats on the disc around the bowl, and draw around them. Drill 6mm (¼in) holes through the disc to line up with the string holes in the cat bases. Attach the handle to the underside of the disk with glue and panel pins.

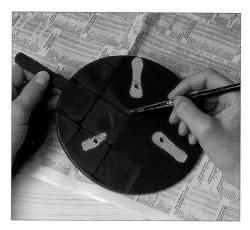

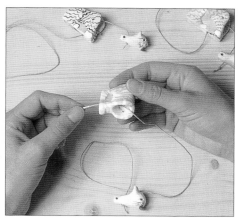

9 Paint each cat differently, giving them form by using coloured stripes, and finish off each character with a painted tongue and face.

10 Seal the wooden base with a coat of white emulsion, avoiding the areas the cats will be glued to. Leave to dry thoroughly. Create the illusion of a tiled floor by using two shades of red, outlining each tile with the darker shade. Varnish when dry.

11 Push the string up through the hole in the base of the cat and into the neck cavity. Now take the string down through the top of the cat's head, securing with a knot below its chin. If the holes prove to be undersize, enlarge them with an appropriate drill.

12 Put the neck into the cavity and secure by pushing a length of copper wire through the holes either side. Seal the ends into the model with a small ball of putty, which when dry, can be retouched before a coat of varnish is applied to the finished models. Push the three strings through the holes in the base and glue into position. Do not get glue into the holes or on the string.

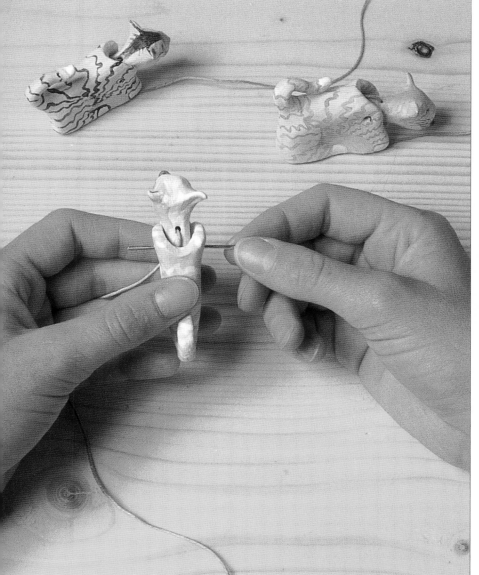

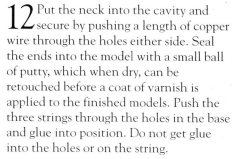

13 Gather the strings together, and thread all three through the pendulum and secure underneath with a knot. To make the cats drink, hold the base by the handle and move your hand in a circular motion.

# MAGNETIC THEATRE

## IN CARD AND MODELLING CLAY

INTERMEDIATE

Create colourful moving characters for your very own stage production. A king and his family set the stage for this royal performance. You may wish to choose your own theme or include characters from a favourite classic tale.

### TOOLS & MATERIALS

- A2 size sheet of coloured mounting board
- Thick coloured cord
- Broad ribbon
- Coloured felt offcuts
- Wooden sticks, 20cm (8in) long
- Gold relief liner
- Double-sided tape
- Split pins

- Plastic modelling clay (Fimo)
- Small round magnets
- Thick dowel, 20cm (8in long)
- Modelling tools
- Craft knife
- Scissors
- Metal ruler
- Cutting mat

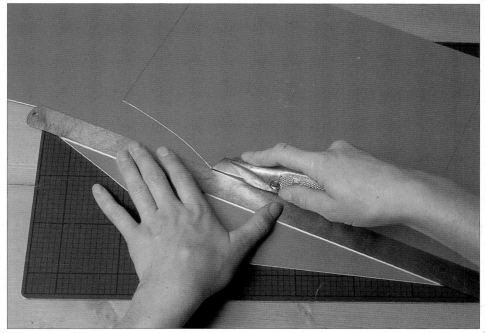

1 Use the measurements from the plan on page 125 to lightly draw the theatre onto a sheet of coloured card. Pay particular attention to which are score lines and which are cuts. Using a sharp knife, metal ruler and cutting mat, cut away the section above the theatre, then gently score the line which will be the front of the stage. From there, cut up the insides of the columns, and round the inside top of the arch, allowing the stage to fold down. Lie the theatre flat again, and gently score the outside edge of the columns. Cut out the slots which will support the stage, then carefully fold back the sides and slot together.

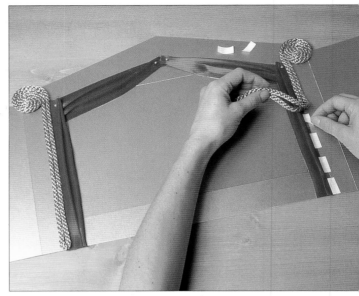

2 Gather the ribbon and drape it on the card to give the impression of curtains. Hold the folds in place by pushing split pins through the ribbon and opening out the backs. Secure the ribbon to the card with small squares of double-sided sticky tape.

3 Fold a length of gold cord in two and lie it alongside the ribbon. Form a coil with the open ends to create the impression of columns. Fix in place with small pieces of double-sided sticky tape.

4 Outline the theatre front with green cord and use small squares of coloured felt to cover the joins of the curtains. Stick all in place with double-sided sticky tape.

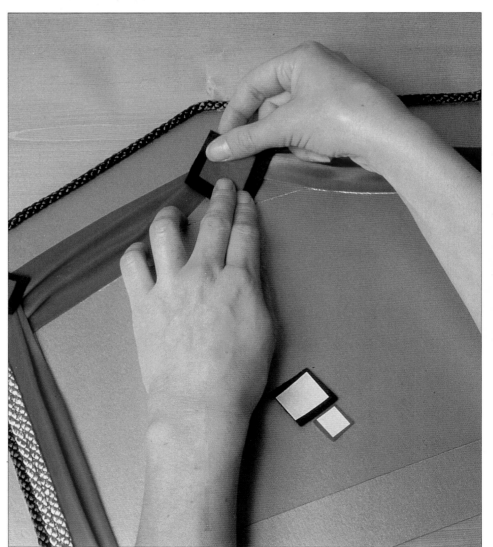

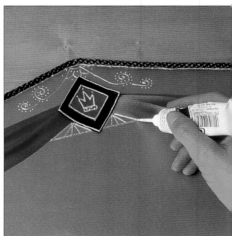

5 Add detail with a gold relief liner to complete the main theatre design. Scenery can be made for whatever production you care to stage, and held in place on the inside flaps with tape.

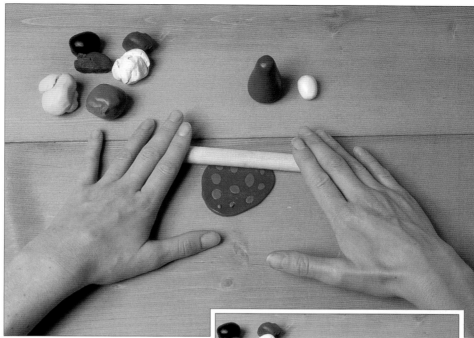

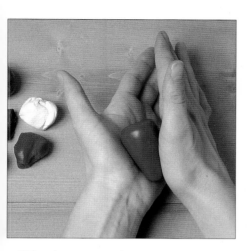

6 The theatre complete, it is time to create the actors. Make a basic body shape by rolling the plastic modelling clay between your palms to form a cone. Use another colour to roll a small ball to make a head.

7 Choose two complementary colours. Roll the first colour flat with a dowel length and add the second by laying small amounts onto the surface and rolling the two together. Cut out a shape from the flattened clay to form a cloak for the character.

8 Mould the clothing onto the body and add details to the head and face with small rolls of colour applied with a modelling tool.

9 Make as many characters as you need for your production, then place them in the oven to harden following the manufacturer's instructions. When they have cooled thoroughly, fix a small magnet to the base of each character with double-sided sticky tape. Attach a magnet to one end of a stick in the same way. The actors glide around the stage, moved from underneath by the sticks.

# THE POLITE PORK BUTCHER

## IN PLYWOOD

INTERMEDIATE

There was a time, before giant supermarkets, when every town had several butcher's shops. One was usually a specialist pork butchers whose trademark was a pig wearing a straw hat and a striped apron. This toy uses a spring clip clothes peg to give the pig two separate movements from one squeeze, jumping and raising the hat.

## TOOLS & MATERIALS

- ◆ Thin card and tracing paper
- ◆ Clothes peg, spring type
- ◆ 3mm (⅛in) plywood, 15cm (6in) square
- ◆ Coathanger wire or similar, 12cm (4¾in) long
- ◆ Four panel pins
- ◆ Glue
- ◆ Small nut
- ◆ Pastel pencils and spray fixative
- ◆ Pencil
- ◆ Fretsaw
- ◆ Pin hammer
- ◆ Sandpaper
- ◆ Pliers
- ◆ Drill
- ◆ Drill bits: 6mm (¼in), same thickness as wire and fine

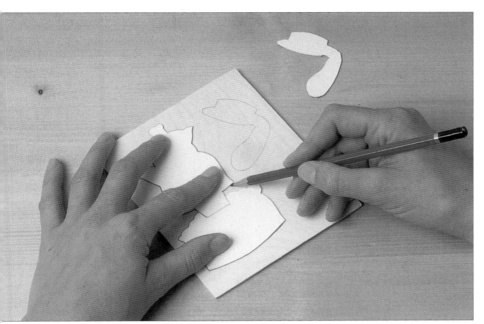

1 Make templates from the trace-offs on page 125. Draw around the outside of the templates onto the 3mm (⅛in) plywood, and add the line that forms the pig's feet. There is no need to mark the holes on these templates, as they do not need to be exact.

2 Cut around the outside shape first, using a fretsaw, before cutting the line that separates the pig from the pie.

3 Gently sand the edges of the plywood clean. Sand the front end of the clothes peg flat, to give as large an area as possible to glue and pin the pig.

4 Use a soft lead pencil to draw the main features onto the pig. Do not be afraid to make mistakes, just sand, or rub until they come off, and re-draw.

5 Pastel pencils give a nice old-fashioned look to the pig and are used here, but paint or coloured pencils will work just as well. Keep the colours simple and do not overwork them or it will end up muddy. Pastels smudge very easily and must be fixed with spray fixative. Alternatively, use several coats of aerosol hair spray, allowing plenty of drying time between each coat.

6 Drill two holes in the arm section, large enough to take the coathanger wire, one for the shoulder joint, the other about 10mm (⅜in) further up the arm. With the same drill, make a hole about 6mm (¼in) from the front end of one half of the peg. Drill a fine pilot hole through the pie front, and into the end of the peg with the wire hole. Glue and pin the pie to the peg. Slot the pig section back into the pie, then drill, glue and pin into position on the remaining side of the peg.

7 Make a 10mm (⅜in) bend in one end of the wire and push through the hole in the peg. Bend it again to point up towards the pig's head. Move 5.5cm (2⅛in) up the wire and bend it back, in the same direction as the peg. Slip the arm on to the wire and establish the best shoulder position by squeezing the peg. Pilot drill the shoulder joint and hammer a panel pin through the hole. Fit the arm using the nut as a spacer between the body and the arm, and finish by bending the pin end back on itself.

8 Bend the wire downwards and cut off the surplus.

# POP-UP BABY

## IN FABRIC

A great favourite with younger children, this puppet can be as simple or as ornate as you like. This one is made with an odd sock. If the other one turns up, make twins!

### TOOLS & MATERIALS

- Thin card, 24cm (9½in) square
- Fabric offcut
- Small child's sock
- 4cm (1⅝in) fibre ball
- Two 16mm (⅝in) fibre balls
- 6mm (¼in) dowel, 40cm (15¾in) long
- Trimmings
- Glue
- Double-sided tape
- Stapler
- Needle and thread
- Ruler
- Compass, pencil
- Scissors
- Pencil sharpener

1 With the compass, draw a 21cm (8¼in) diameter circle onto the card. Divide the circle in half by drawing a line through the centre and add a 16mm (⅝in) tab to half the width. Cut out the semi-circle with the tab on and use it as the pattern for the fabric cone cover, adding 19mm (¾in) to the curved edge.

2 Cut out the fabric cone cover and put to one side until needed. Stick double-sided sticky tape onto the inside of the tab on the card semi-circle, pull into a cone shape, and stick together.

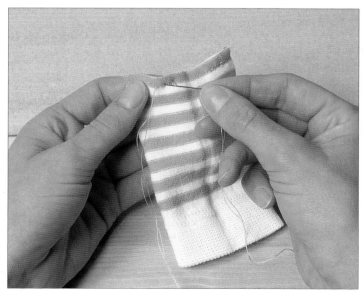

3 Make the body by cutting off the leg of the sock. Turn the piece inside out. Use a needle and thread or staples to close the cut edge, leaving a small neck hole in the centre.

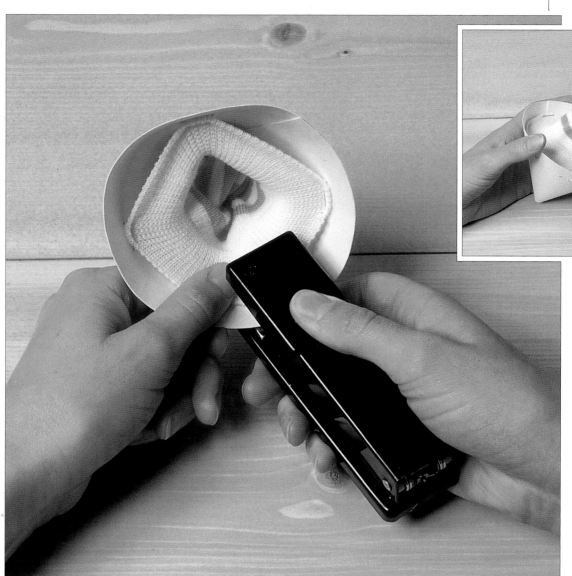

4 Fix the body tube into the cone with staples. Staple opposite sides, easing the sock on as you go until it is joined all around. Pull the sock up.

5 Fold the fabric for the cone cover in half, right sides together to form a triangle, and staple down the seam. Turn it right side out and slip over the cone. Run a generous bead of glue around the inside edge of the card and tuck the fabric in as neatly as possible.

6 Sharpen one end of the dowel with a pencil sharpener. Push the sharpened end up through the base of the cone and out through the neck hole. Glue the head onto the point of the dowel. Glue the body firmly underneath the head.

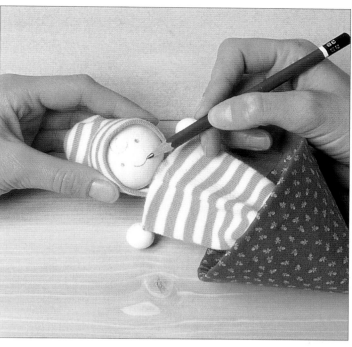

7 Cut the heel and toe off what remains of the sock, and use this to make the hat. Reduce to the size of the head if necessary by seaming down the length. Make a running stitch across one end, and pull tight to gather it. Hem the other end and glue into position on the head.

8 Sew the small balls firmly in place onto the end of the shoulder seams. Use a soft pencil to draw on a face, this can easily be rubbed out if the first attempt looks more like the elephant man.

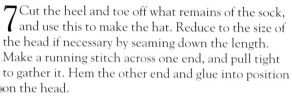

9 Finish off by gluing trimmings on to the inside edge of the cone to cover any untidy edges. Cup the cone in one hand and holding the stick in the other, pull down, the baby disappears, push up and it pops back up. Twist it from side to side, and the baby turns too.

# FLYING PIG

## IN CARD

Pigs really do fly when you follow these simple instructions. Of course you don't have to make a pig, any creature of similar proportions will work equally well. You could also try cutting the shapes from wood for a more robust toy.

EASY

## TOOLS & MATERIALS

- Tracing paper
- Thick card 18 x 20cm (7⅛ x 8in)
- 70cm (27½in) of cord or string
- 10cm (4in) of elastic cord
- Pencil
- Pink water-based paint
- Water-based varnish
- Grey and gold relief liners
- Two split pins
- Fine sandpaper
- Scissors
- Bradawl or hole punch
- Artist's brushes

1 Trace the body and wing shapes on page 126 on to the thick card. Remember to mark the holes and to draw two wings. Cut out the shapes with a pair of sharp scissors.

2 Pierce string size holes where the pencil marks fall using a bradawl or hole punch. Lightly sand around the edges to give a smooth finish to each shape.

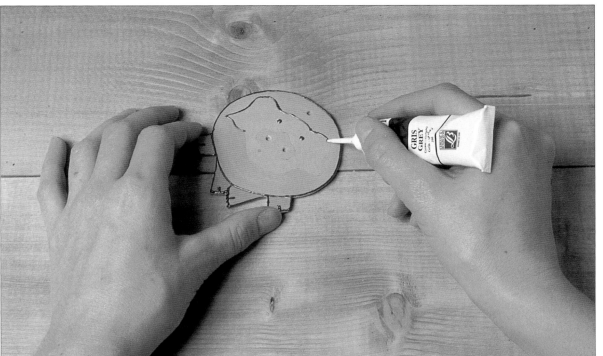

3 Paint the body of the pig pink, allow to dry, then apply a coat of varnish to the wings and the body to strengthen them. Use a pencil to sketch an outline of the head and ears, using the two holes in the centre as nostrils. When satisfied with the drawing, use a grey relief liner to draw in the features.

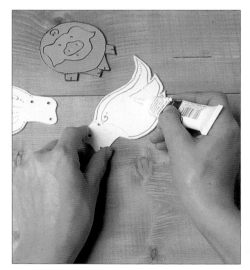

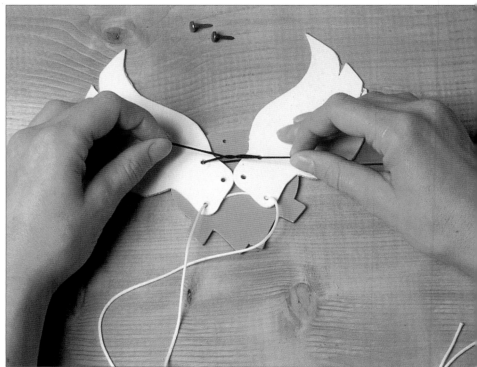

4 Decorate the wings with a gold relief liner and leave to dry.

5 Thread the string through the lowest hole on each wing. Thread the elastic through the two top holes. Rest the wings on the reverse side of the body and line up the two middle holes with the nostrils. Use this as a guideline to judge the length of elastic required to keep the wings in an upright position. Once satisfied, secure the elastic with a knot. Tie the two ends of string loosely together and pull to create a slight tension in the elastic, and tie off. Wrap one end of the string over the knot and tie again below it, ensuring that when pulled, the strings will not slide off-centre.

**6** Push the two split pins through the nostrils and wing holes from the front and open out the pin backs.

**7** Fold a piece of string in half and push the looped end through the hole at the top of the body. Thread the two ends through the loop and pull tightly. Tie together with a slip knot. Hang up your pig and gently tug the pullstring to see him fly.

# THE JUMPING DOG

## IN FIBRE BOARD

This toy is a pastiche of life in our garden. Jeffrey, our ginger tomcat, torments Pattie, our terrier, by sitting for hours just out of reach while Pattie tries to jump up and see what the attraction is. Pattie's only reward is an occasional slap on the head from her very aloof best friend Jeffrey.

## TOOLS & MATERIALS

- Thin card and tracing paper
- Two 6mm (¼in) plywood 9cm (3½in) square
- 6mm (¼in) MDF, 32 x 14cm (12⅝ x 5½in) for backplate
- 12mm (½in) MDF, 14cm (5½in) square
- 6mm (¼in) dowel, 3cm (1⅛in) long
- Wooden ball
- Cord or string, 30cm (12in)
- Two small eyelets
- Six small panel pins
- Double-sided tape
- Masking tape
- Craft knife
- White emulsion paint
- Acrylic paints
- Gloss varnish
- Glue
- Pencil
- Soft lead pencil
- Ruler
- Protective mask and goggles
- Fretsaw
- Clamp
- Drill
- Drill bits: to match dowel and fine
- Artist's brushes
- Blunt knife
- Cloth

1 Make card templates for the backplate, dog's body and legs from the trace-offs on pages 126 – 127. Tape the two 9cm (3½in) squares of plywood together with double-sided sticky tape. Use the templates to draw out all the components, taking care to mark the hole positions.

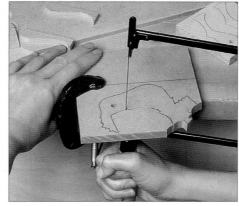

2 Put on the mask. Drill a 6mm (¼in) hole through the plywood rear leg section, and a 6mm (¼in) hole through the hip position on the dog's body. Clamp the workpiece to the bench and cut out all the parts with a fretsaw.

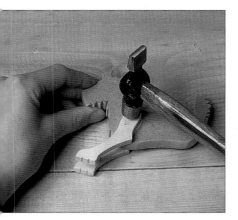

3 Separate the taped legs by easing apart with a blunt knife. Attach the front legs to the body with glue and two panel pins each side. The legs need to be securely fixed as they have to absorb a shock every time the dog lands.

4 Position the ground on the backplate about 6cm (2⅜in) up from the bottom and secure with glue and two panel pins nailed from behind. Leave the glue to dry before painting all parts with an undercoat of white emulsion paint.

5 Mark out the cat's features in pencil on to the backplate. Block out the shape of the fence with masking tape. Cut around and remove the tape from the cat and the fence cross pieces with a craft knife. Use a drill slightly wider than the cord to make two small holes, to wall-mount the toy, one in the centre under the ground shelf, the other top centre, avoiding the cat. Drill a hole through the wooden ball.

6 To paint the cat, put some paints into a small dish, and pick up more than one colour on the brush at a time. Painting wet into wet will help the colours bleed into one another and give an impression of fur. Play around until you are happy with the cat colour then leave it to dry – the detail will be put on later. If the painting goes wrong, simply wash it off and try again.

7 Use two or three different greens to paint a variety of leaf shapes and sizes all over the background. Allow to dry, then paint in some flowers using bright, bold colours.

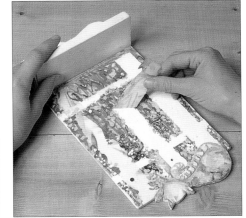

8 When the paint is thoroughly dry, gently peal back the masking tape. Do not be alarmed if the paint has bled slightly under the edges of the tape, it will still look like foliage when the toy is completed.

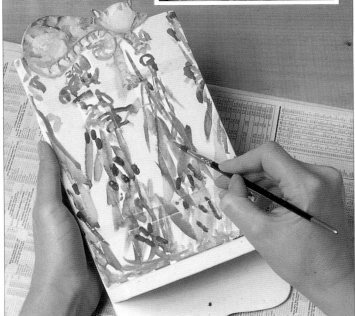

9 Colourwash all the remaining primed surfaces with diluted green paint, applied freely with a wet cloth.

**10** Using a soft pencil and ruler, outline the fence then draw the eyes, nose, whiskers and so on onto the cat. Paint a flower or two in front of the fence, and add any finishing touches to the cat. When thoroughly dry, finish with a coat of gloss varnish.

**11** Paint the dog with black and white paints, mixed on your palette to give a variety of greys. Use strong brushstrokes following the lines the dog's coat would take, and finish by painting in the eye and any highlights in white. Allow to dry before applying a coat of varnish.

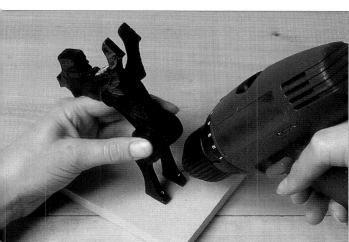

**12** Glue the dowel into the hole in one leg. Pass the dowel through the hip joint and glue on the other leg. Drill a pilot hole in each of the back feet, and glue and panel pin the dog on to the ground plate.

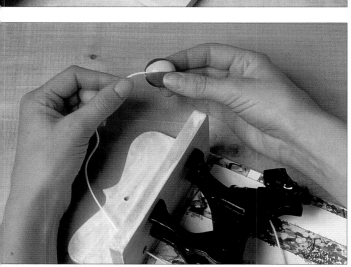

**13** Drill a pilot hole, and screw a small eyelet into the back of the dog's neck, roughly where the collar would be. Screw the other eyelet onto the fence, slightly higher then the one on the dog when the dog is standing on his hind legs. Drill a 6mm (¼in) hole through the ground plate directly below the eyelet on the fence. Tie one end of the cord to the eyelet on the dog, feed it through the eyelet on the fence, and down through the hole in the ground, attaching it to the painted ball. Seal both knots with a spot of glue.

# TEMPLATES

The trace-off shapes given on these pages are the same size as used in the projects. The only exception is the Magnetic Theatre which has a plan showing the theatre's dimensions. There is also a plan to show how to cut and fold the sculptor's mesh for the Spinning Harlequin. To find out how to make a template, turn to Materials, Tools and Techniques page 15.

ZOETROPE
*pages 28 – 31*

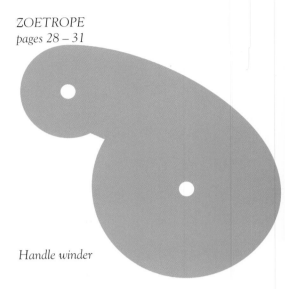

*Handle winder*

*Slots and scallops*

TRADITIONAL CAROUSEL
*pages 22 – 27*

*Horse*

*Canopy*

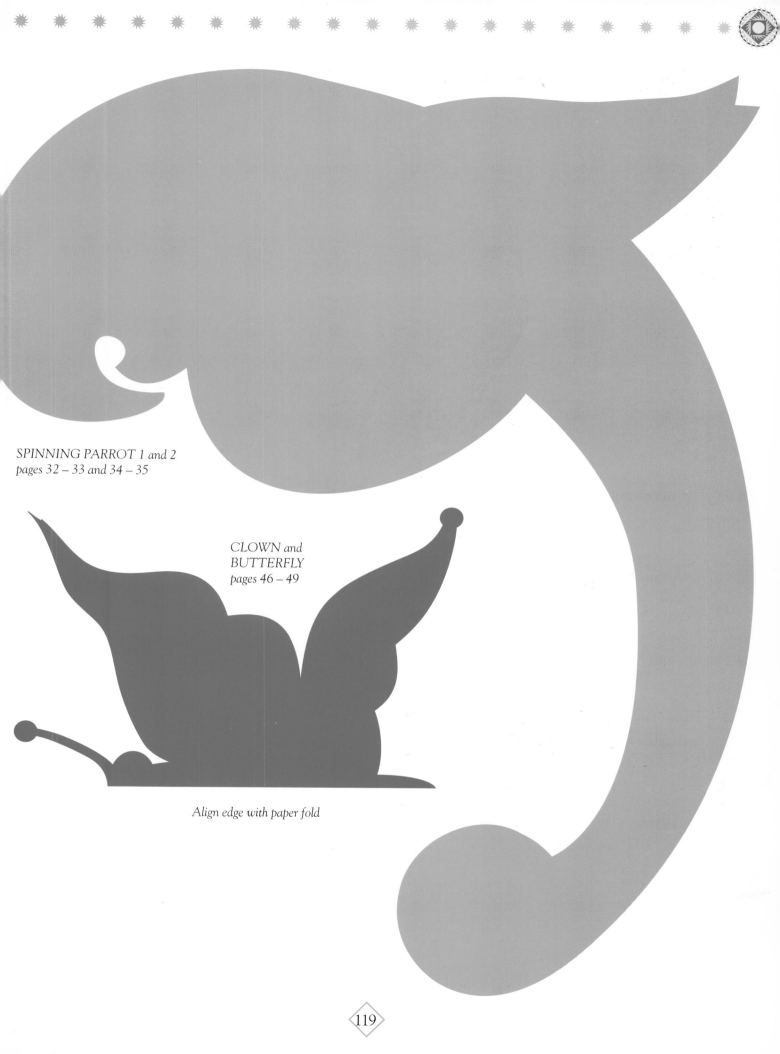

*SPINNING PARROT 1 and 2*
*pages 32 – 33 and 34 – 35*

*CLOWN and*
*BUTTERFLY*
*pages 46 – 49*

*Align edge with paper fold*

SWIMMING DOLPHINS
pages 36 – 41

*Dolphin*

*Wave*
Trace the outline on this page, then
slide the tracing paper right until
your pencil marks butt up against
the outline on page 121, using the
dotted lines as a guide. Complete
the tracing.

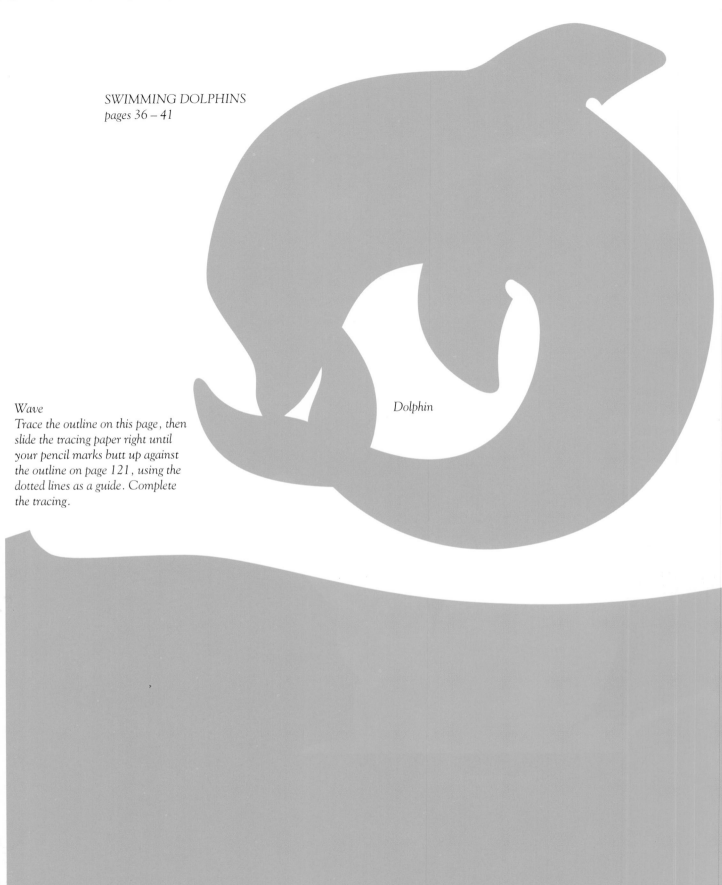

*FALLING MONKEY*
*pages 56 – 57*

CLIMBING MONKEY
*pages 52 – 55*

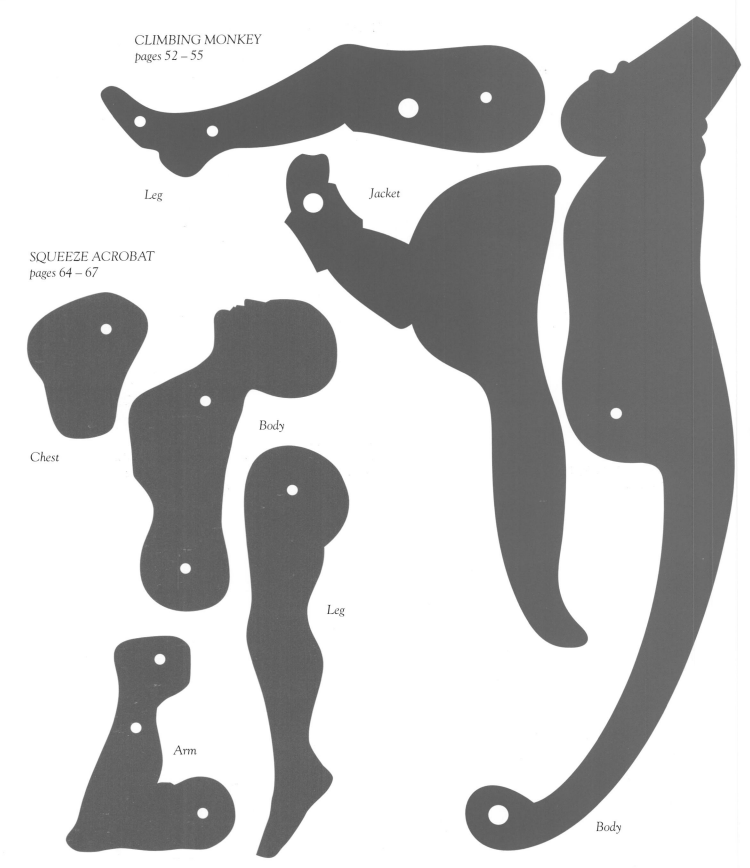

Leg

Jacket

SQUEEZE ACROBAT
*pages 64 – 67*

Chest

Body

Body

Leg

Arm

Body

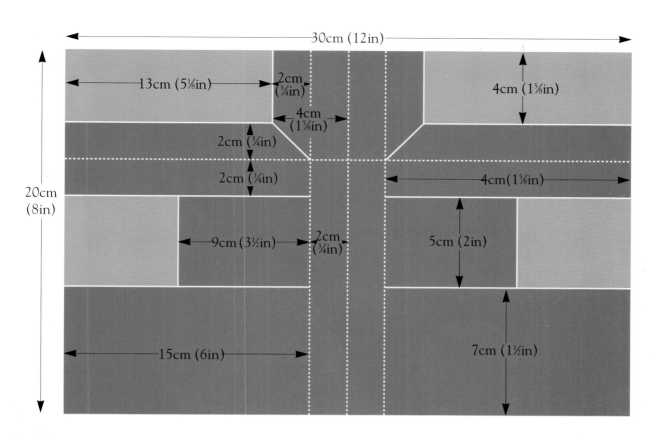

SPINNING HARLEQUIN
pages 74 – 79

Plan for sculptor's mesh
In the diagram above, the dots indicate fold lines and the solid lines where to cut. The red areas are the parts of the mesh used in the figure, and the orange areas sections cut away.

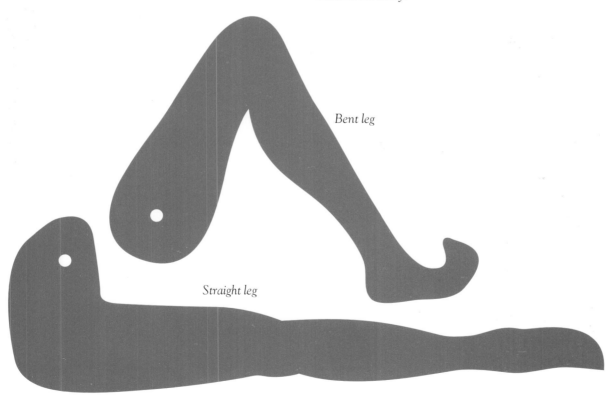

Bent leg

Straight leg

THE
WOODCUTTER
*pages 82 – 87*

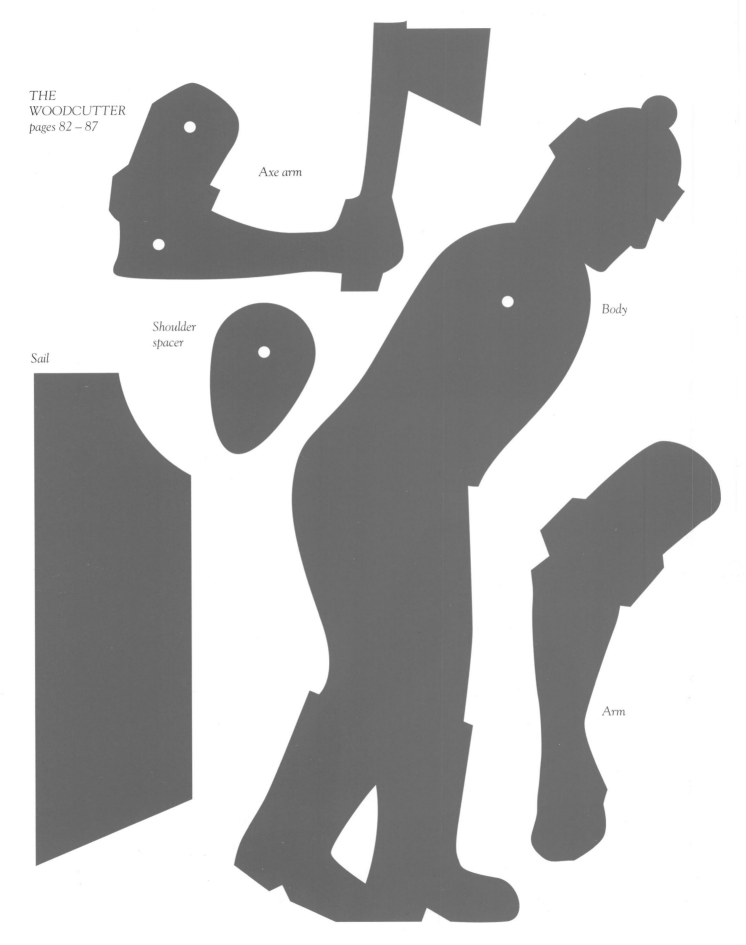

Axe arm

Shoulder
spacer

Sail

Body

Arm

20cm
(8in)

42cm
(16⅝in)

20cm
(8in)

8cm
(3⅛in)

30cm
(12in)

24cm
(9½in)

16cm (6¼in)

20cm
(8in)

9cm (3½in)

*THE POLITE PORK BUTCHER*
*pages 102 – 105*

*Arm*

*Body*

*MAGNETIC THEATRE*
*pages 98 – 101*
*In the diagram left, the dots indicate fold lines and the solid lines where to cut. The pale green area is cut out on three sides and folded back as indicated by the bottom dotted line.*

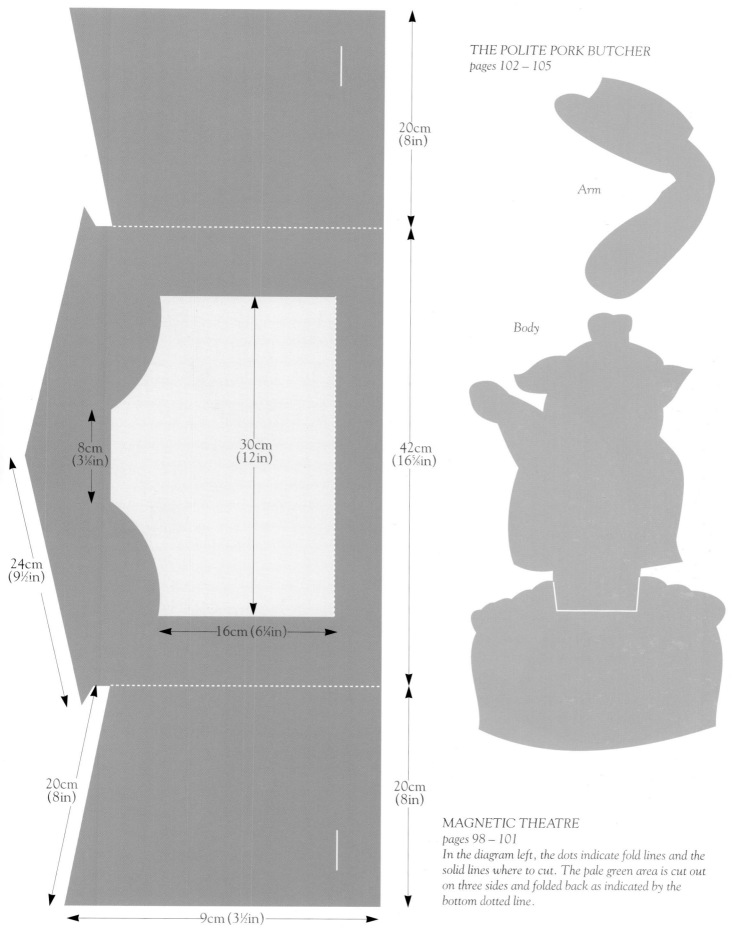

## THE JUMPING DOG
*pages 114 – 117*
*Trace the outline on this page, then slide the tracing paper right until your pencil marks butt up against the outline on page 127, using the dotted lines as a guide. Complete the tracing. On another piece of paper, trace around the light blue shapes of the dog to make its templates.*

Back plate

## FLYING PIG
*pages 110 – 113*

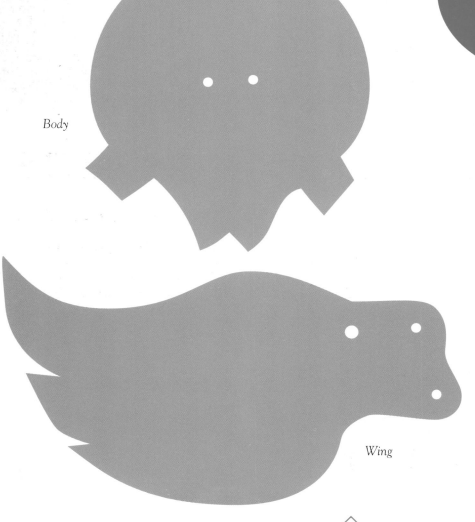

Body

Wing

Dog's body

Dog's back leg

Dog's front leg

# SUPPLIERS & ACKNOWLEDGEMENTS

## SUPPLIERS

When making the toys we have taken care to use materials and equipment which are widely and easily available. You will therefore find nearly all the things you need in your local stationers, art and craft or DIY stores.

### Art and sculpting materials

Daler Rowney stock a wide range of art materials nationwide. Call 0171 636 8241 for stockists and mail order information.

Alec Tiranti Ltd stock sculpting tools and materials including sculptor's mesh. Call 0118 930 2775 for mail order.

Paperchase offer a wide range of papers from around the world and stock art materials. Call 0171 580 8496 to find out your nearest branch or for mail order call 0171 323 3707.

### DIY stores

Do It All stock a wide range of DIY tools and materials nationwide. Call 0800 436 436 to find out your nearest branch.

B & Q stock a wide range of DIY tools and materials nationwide. Call 0181 466 4166 to find out your nearest branch and further information on products stocked.

## ACKNOWLEDGEMENTS

Our tools have been with us a long time and hence were far too scratched and battered to be used in the photographs for the book. We would therefore like to thank Bosch for lending us the power tools featured in the book.

# INDEX